LIVING A PURPOSE-FULL LIFE

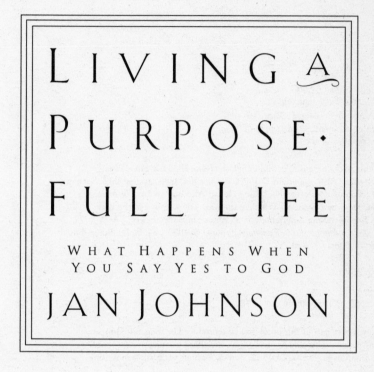

LIVING A PURPOSE-FULL LIFE

WHAT HAPPENS WHEN YOU SAY YES TO GOD

JAN JOHNSON

WATERBROOK
PRESS

LIVING A PURPOSE-FULL LIFE
PUBLISHED BY WATERBROOK PRESS
5446 North Academy Boulevard, Suite 200
Colorado Springs, Colorado 80918
A division of Random House, Inc.

ISBN 1-57856-048-9

Library of Congress Cataloging-in-Publication Data
Johnson, Jan, 1947–
    Living a purpose-full life : what happens when you say yes to
God / Jan Johnson.—1st ed.
      p.   cm.
    ISBN 1-57856-048-9
    1. Christian women—Religious life.   I. Title.
BV4527.J635 1999
248.8'43—dc21   98-50854
                                                CIP

Printed in the United States of America

1999

10 9 8 7 6 5 4 3 2

CONTENTS

ACKNOWLEDGMENTS

Thanks goes, as always, to Greg Johnson, who reads nearly everything I write and is a writer's dream of a husband as a skillful editor and affirmer. Thanks also to my writer-friend Ranelda Hunsicker, who read this manuscript, asked me difficult questions, and gave me great suggestions. She and Kay Lindskoog helped me think through biblical perspectives on self-worth. I also thank my editor, Liz Heaney, who helped birth the idea for this book and persuaded me to give it shape in ways I could never have conceived by myself.

My thanks and admiration go to the women who allowed me to interview them for this book: Miriam Adeney, Toni Baldwin, JoeAnn Ballard, Elaine Barsness, Sandy Burgess, Evelyn Curtiss, Sheila Lichacz, Elsie Purnell, Christina Riccardi, and Christine Sine. Their stories and insights have taught me more about what it means to be a woman with purpose and have created for me pictures that will stay with me for the rest of my life.

Hungry for Purpose

Have you ever had one of those hectic days when you wondered, *Would the disciples have run their lives with daily planners in little loose-leaf notebooks?* You've crossed off the errands on your to-do list and you've made all those telephone calls, but you wonder, *Did God intend for my life to be so frantic?*

Or perhaps you've found yourself having more life-defining moments, sitting in places such as hospital waiting rooms and wondering, *Has my life counted for anything? Have I made a difference for someone else?*

These two crosscurrents—too much activity and too little meaning—have created a floating dissatisfaction among many women. The first is a surging torrent of morning-noon-and-night busyness while the other is a quiet ticking away of life's minutes without purpose. These two processes can prompt a penetrating self-examination: *Why am I doing these things? What is all this for?*

If that's how you feel, you are not alone. While interviewing many women for this book and staying up late talking to others at retreats, I've heard varied questions and comments regarding purpose in life, such as:

- "I don't really like my job, but what can I do?"
- "There's so much I'd like to do—how do I decide?"
- "I may be fifty, but I'm still trying to decide what to be when I grow up."

Linda, for example, has achieved her career goal of becoming a nurse manager, and although she's a competent one, she feels something is missing. She considered going to medical school to become a doctor. "But I thought about it and figured out it was only so I could own a luxurious home and have more people look up to me.

"It all eludes me. I go to church and read my Bible, but I don't make a difference in this world. After a wasted evening of unplanned television watching, I feel guilty. Sure, I'm nice enough to fill in for other nurses when they have a sick kid at home, but I don't ever go the extra mile as Jesus said to. My work is my work and my faith is my faith. Patients represent more things to do, not people with souls that God loves."

Things came to a head when Linda attended her twenty-year high school reunion. "I saw my life was ticking away. I have only a certain amount of time left. I want to do the things I thought were meaningful. Is what I'm doing still meaningful to me? I've got to figure that out."

Denise is at home with three children and enjoys the comings and goings of a mom's life. But in the quiet moments, as she rocks her crying toddler, she wonders if the latchkey kids down the street can operate the microwave without burning themselves. She thinks about the bag lady who was digging scraps out of the dumpster at the fast-food restaurant and wonders where she sleeps. "Yes," she says, "I'm taking care of my kids, but isn't there something we could do together to be like Jesus?"

Mary began working as a bank teller years ago because "I didn't want to think about my job after hours, so I'd be free to focus on my husband and kids." Even though her children are now grown, her after-work hours are filled with running from one activity to another—picking up prescriptions, going to church meetings. She didn't think much about purpose until her friend's son was diagnosed with AIDS and Mary helped care for him. After he died, she attended a grief support group with her friend. "They helped each other so much—I envied that," Mary commented. "I do good things, but is anyone's life better because of what I've done?"

One night after giving a dinner party to entertain the big kahunas from her husband's office, Mary became almost angry as she cleaned up. "Where am I going in life?" she asked her husband. "Yes, I care for you and I enjoy my job. But I want something to live and die for besides a clean kitchen counter and a car that's fun to drive. We haven't made it this long together to do nothing, have we?"

Women from twenty to seventy, single and married, are searching for meaning in the midst of their nonstop coming and going. Sometimes this questioning is spurred by decade birthdays—thirty, forty, fifty, sixty, seventy—or by an event such as a reunion at which we suddenly realize life is not a dress rehearsal. Sometimes it's triggered by a loss or a failure: divorce, children leaving home, long-term unemployment, a mastectomy, or the death of a parent. That catastrophe creates a space in our lives, and we realize we're not willing to go back to the hectic way things were.

Achievement can spawn introspection as well. A successful certified public accountant working for a large firm told me: "When I chose this field, I was an insecure, bleached-blond nineteen-year-old. I've achieved her goals and it wasn't such a big deal after all. What will I do now?" Another woman whose last child was leaving home said to me, "Will I ever find anything as meaningful as parenting my children?"

IS GETTING OUT OF THE HOUSE THE ANSWER?

Especially since the onset of the women's movement, women have broken barriers and defied discrimination. When I was young, girls who wrote to NASA asking what it would take to become an astronaut were informed that girls need not apply. In the decades since, NASA has said to women, "Please do apply!" If barriers have melted, why has the level of dissatisfaction remained the same?

Getting out of the house is not the definitive road to fulfillment because even if she leaves home, a woman is not guaranteed meaningful work. A study presented in the *Journal of Organizational Behavior* confirmed the notion that women have higher job-turnover rates than men. A survey of nearly six hundred male and female executives, managers, and professionals revealed that women were twice as likely as men to leave their jobs within two years (22.2 percent of the women versus 12.2 percent of the men).

Why do women change jobs or leave the work force so frequently? The study looked at reasons such as wages, tenure, benefits, working conditions, job security, and paid vacation. As I examined this study, I assumed women left jobs to avoid discrimination, to stay home with their kids, or to glide in the "mommy track" (working fewer hours or less-demanding jobs). I was wrong. According to the survey, the primary reason women quit their jobs was lack of satisfaction with the job itself. This study, described in an article aptly titled, "Ain't Got No Satisfaction: Working Women," shows women often don't find their jobs meaningful and they're rankled by that.[1] While income is important, a paycheck is not enough to hold many women to a particular job.

In fact, the trend of women joining the work force is reversing itself.[2] In describing the phenomenon of increasing numbers of women leaving the work force, author Leith Anderson told this story in *Christianity Today*:

> Karol Emmerich, 45, was listed by *Working Woman* magazine
> as one of 73 female executives "ready to run corporate
> America." As vice president, treasurer, and chief accounting
> officer of the Dayton Hudson Corporation, she became the
> highest-level woman in the $18 billion retailing company.
> Then, in May 1993, she resigned to pursue community-service
> projects and offer her expertise to Christian organizations. Said
> Emmerich, "I recognize that career advancement is not going
> to fill all the needs in my life." She says she is after a "more
> balanced life" where she can focus on "nurturing relation-
> ships—with God, my family, old and new friends."[3]

Even in a top-level job, certain things are missing that women want from life: meaningful partnership in God's purposes, connectedness with others, making a difference in this world. Better jobs and more respect haven't brought us what we want. Instead, we have discovered that materialism breeds discontent, trying to be superwomen breeds fragmentation, and working in an office (even a church office) staffed by people with large egos breeds disillusionment.

This search for meaning is so pervasive that "legacy coach" (a combination of mentor, taskmaster, motivational speaker, business consultant, and therapist) was the runner-up hottest consulting track in 1996, according to *U.S. News & World Report*.[4] Those hiring coaches include women looking not only for career counseling, but also seeking direction and meaning in life. Amy Watson of Coach University (a Houston-based classroom-without-walls founded in 1992) tells about a female university professor who was overwhelmed with the demands of life, especially teaching and publishing responsibilities. She hired a "legacy coach" to figure out which projects were most crucial to her, which she could let go, which tasks to delegate to colleagues, and how to manage her work load.[5] Like her, many of us are trying to figure out what is most important and how to arrange our lives around that.

Women who stay at home with children face similar struggles. They understand that one of their life purposes is nurturing children, but the long-term picture is fuzzy. Changing diapers and cleaning up messes, when done with love, make a huge difference. Yet these women desire to do as women throughout the ages have done—be mothers *and* obey the commands of God to be a light to God's world in some way (Matthew 28:19-20; 1 Timothy 4:10-11).

SOMETHING BIGGER THAN ME

All these women are crying out for a purpose in life, or what may be referred to as a "sense of mission" or a "calling." Our purpose in life is a narrow slice of God's enormous purposes. For example, the apostle Paul had one single-minded mission: "Although I am less than the least of all God's people, this grace was given me: to preach to the Gentiles the unsearchable riches of Christ" (Ephesians 3:8). But purpose in life is more than a task to do. Paul didn't just preach; he did whatever was necessary to win a people for whom his heart was broken—the Gentiles (Galatians 1:16; 2:2, 8; Ephesians 3:1; 2 Timothy 4:17). Like Paul, Peter also had that special mission of establishing the church, but his ministry was geared primarily to the Jewish world. Obviously, the same specific purpose may be lived out in many ways, depending on an individual's opportunities, temperament, and relationships.

Some women may be unable to articulate their purpose, but it runs through their lives thematically, woven through their tasks and relationships on a daily basis as a red thread spanning the length of a garment. When I asked my friend Barbara Dauer about her purpose, she could not identify it, but I've watched her for years, and it's obvious to me: She educates the have-nots in our culture.

When I first met Barbara, in addition to her part-time job, she was befriending Cambodian refugees and teaching them English as a second language. When she later began teaching kindergarten, it wasn't long before she was asked to teach the "wise 5s class"—a prekindergarten class for children who "had not" the readiness for academic kindergarten. A few years later, she was offered a job at an inner-city school. Since I'd lived in that area, she asked me, "Is it a safe neighborhood?" I told her it absolutely was not safe and drive-by shootings were common. "But this neighborhood is filled with people of great courage, overcoming obstacles you and I will never experience," I added. "Living there gave me the courage to begin writing." Even though Barbara has had to work hard at overcoming fears in her life, she took the job. Show this woman a marginalized, ill-thought-of person, and she'll wonder how she can teach him or her to read and write.

Our purposes in life answer our unfulfilled longings to communicate what we believe is important or to change the things about the world that break our heart. When we don't pay attention to these longings, we feel empty and isolated, no matter how well paid, well loved, or well coifed we are.

If you sense the heartbreak of God and cannot express it, you will be frustrated. This appears to have been the case with Elizabeth Dole several years ago. Based on what she has said and done, one of her life purposes appears to be improving conditions for those in need. As secretary of labor in the early 1990s, she prepared a massive initiative to prevent abuse of farm workers and improve their working conditions. In her plan she wrote: "I was shocked and deeply moved by what I witnessed [when touring the fields]. I saw conditions that are not only unnecessary and unacceptable for any workers, but also are an affront to human dignity." Her initiative was rebuffed, however, and so conditions remained unchanged. A labor source familiar with the plan said that it was a factor in her resignation four months later.[6] When Mrs. Dole went on to become president of the American Red Cross, I was not surprised. This is a woman who obviously has a heart for the hurting, and she chose a job in which she could express that fully.

Our bond with God is such a deep one—being created in his image— that we won't find meaning except in him (Genesis 1:26-27). The apostle Paul described this pull toward God: "Men would seek him and perhaps reach out for him and find him, though he is not far from each one of us. 'For in him we live and move and have our being.' As some of your own poets have said, 'We are his offspring'" (Acts 17:27-28). Depend upon this truth: We—as God's offspring, living and moving and having our being in him—can expect to feel lost when we are out of relationship with God or existing outside his purposes. We were created for a love relationship with God, and in that relationship we are inspired to fulfill his purposes. If we don't know Christ or make him known, we will long to do so.

That's why a purpose-full life must be lived in conversation with God. Through that conversation, we fall in sync with God's purposes. When we've done this, no one has to ask us to do something within our purpose because we will have already gotten involved or started asking questions about it.

The benefits of giving ourselves to purpose-full living are enormous. We stop wondering what we should be doing and start looking for time to do what tugs at our thoughts. We look forward to today's tasks because they're more likely to be related to our purposes. We feel our contribution is respected and appreciated—maybe not by the world at large or by the next-door neighbor or by anybody at church. But we know these tasks are linked to God's purposes and are, therefore, important and worthy of respect. When describing the work to others, we emanate satisfaction and appropriate pride because, as Frank Laubach says, we have a sense of God's hand reaching back to lead us while his other hand stretches forth unseen into his will.[7]

Doing What God Created Me to Do

As a woman staying at home with my preschoolers, I knew what I was doing was important, but I longed for God to use me in other ways too. One of my joys was teaching teenagers in the urban church where my husband pastored. I worked hard to help kids see how relevant and exciting the Bible is. (I would later state this purpose at the top of my résumé as, "making the Bible come alive.") Surviving in a teenage Sunday school classroom with a mixture of several languages and nationalities wasn't easy. My college degree in Christian education wasn't cutting it, so I attended workshops on how to make learning fun for my teenage students. Through one of those workshops, I was invited by an editor to submit samples of how I adapted the publisher's lessons to fit my urban teenagers. The thought terrified me so much that I didn't send them anything until a few years later when I was turning thirty. I remember thinking, *Gee, my life is going to be over soon. If I'm ever going to write curriculum, I'd better do it now!* (Yes, I thought this at thirty!) My lesson plans were soon published.

So during my kids' preschool years, I spent their naps writing Bible study curriculum for teenagers. (No, my kids didn't sleep perfectly each time, but they had a few "bed toys" to keep them content.) For two hours a day, I entered another world in which I hashed out biblical principles, bonded with Bible figures, and plotted how to make them live in the minds of kids whose parents were divorcing, dying, or unknown, and who were afraid to use the bathroom at school because they might be jumped. When my own kids' naps ended, I was terribly drained and terribly refreshed.

When someone important to me minimized my work one day—"So you're writing those little teacher's books"—I explained what writing curriculum meant to me. I saw myself going unseen into classrooms around the nation, helping teachers motivate confused teens and introduce them to a down-to-earth but high and holy Savior who loves them just as they are. As I finished, my listener rolled his eyes, and I felt embarrassed for speaking with such passion. Yet it also felt right. I knew I was doing one of the things God had created me to do. I knew I was entering territory that had something to do with my purposes in life, although they weren't yet clear to me.

Now, fifteen years later, people ask me if I've "gotten past writing curriculum" because I've also written books and magazine articles. I try to explain more calmly why I love curriculum writing. Writing Bible study curriculum wasn't just a smart career move to bring in enough money to buy a computer. It grew out of a passion born in me as a child. On Saturdays I went to bars with my dad, and on Sundays I went to church with my mother. I often imagined the Jesus I heard about on Sunday being authentic enough to mingle with, eat with, and befriend the people I met on Saturday at the Oasis Café. When I write those "little teacher's books" (for adults now), I imagine class members struggling with every possible hurt and sin—greed, illness, bankruptcy, snobbishness—and I try to equip their teacher to make God come alive to them.

As time has passed and I've begun speaking at retreats, I've mentioned this idea of purpose in life and received several reactions: blank stares from those who have never considered they might have a purpose; "aha" expressions from those who were once inflamed with purpose but let it go; knowing looks, beaming grins, and hearty handshakes from those who have a sense of God's hand upon them and can't believe that someone is putting into words this unspeakable feeling. Participating in this adventure of living a purpose-full life drives us to God over and over, asking him questions and seeking his face. It forces us to look outside ourselves to the world God *so loved* (John 3:16) and ask God what it would mean for us to live as Jesus Christ did while he walked on this planet.

My twenty-year-plus journey of purpose and my interaction with people, especially women, has led me to write this book, hoping that readers will seek God for their purposes in life. I've seen discontent women be transformed when they are filled with God and partnering with him for eternal purposes. This book is about that journey and speaks to women at different places along the way. In the first section, "A Purpose-Full Life," I'll clarify what does and does not constitute purpose in life, what God's purposes are on this earth, and whether women have a part in that. In the second section, "Uncovering Your Purposes," we'll go about the gritty work of recognizing the purposes already existing within us, but which may seem fuzzy or unrecognizable. In the third section, "Moving Down the Road," we'll talk about the foundational processes needed in pursuing purposes. If you feel thwarted, one of these issues may be holding you back. In the last section, "Staying on Track," we'll look at the snafus we encounter in pursuing our purposes in life. How can we focus on God-given purposes when everything around us would pull us away?

At the close of each chapter, I've included questions to help you ponder what this material means to your life. You may wish to use these for journaling or for exploring with a friend. And you'll want to try each "Experiment in Listening Prayer," laying the specified questions before God as you walk or drive or wipe off the kitchen counter. I believe you'll be surprised at the answers that come to you in the silence and throughout the day. I've also included specific Bible passages that touch on the theme of each chapter. I hope you'll spend some time reflecting on these verses and considering what God might be saying to you through his Word regarding your purpose.

The Bible studies at the back of this book will help you delve even deeper into what God wants you to know about his purposes, and I hope you'll find insight and direction as you prayerfully work your way through his Word. In each phase of the journey of purpose, the thing that makes it interesting—and keeps it from being overwhelmingly scary—is the rich and surprising interaction with God.

QUESTIONS TO PONDER OR DISCUSS

1. Have you envied someone who seems to have a sense of purpose? If so, what exactly did you envy?
2. Who are some of the women you most admire? Why?
3. As you think about the activities on which you place high priority, where do you see yourself on the chart below? Keep in mind that the terms *surviving, searching,* and *being* don't refer to how much money is made but to the attitude with which a job is done, whether it be mothering or running a corporation.[8]

SURVIVING

- Looks for money, status, approval, or prestige
- Motivated by greed or workaholism
- Driven by fear, anxiety, inadequacy
- Swings from *I'll make it no matter what* to *What's to become of me?*

SEARCHING

- Wonders, *Is this possible for me? Can I do it? Do I dare?*
- Finds a fit between own interests and wants of others
- Enjoys self-improvement
- Engages in long-term strategic planning
- Feels "divine dissatisfaction"; is restless; suffers mood swings; wants a road map now!

BEING

- Cares for the greater good
- Feels she was born to do this
- Experiences joy, creativity, courage in work
- Is confident
- Able to ask for what she wants

EXPERIMENT IN LISTENING PRAYER

Ask God, *What events or feelings prompt me to daydream about purpose or to itch with discontent?*

BIBLE PASSAGE TO CONTEMPLATE

Sit quietly and reflect on 1 Timothy 4:12,14. What words or phrases most speak to you?

> Don't let anyone look down on you because you are young, but set an example for the believers in speech, in life, in love, in faith and in purity.... Do not neglect your gift, which was given you through a prophetic message when the body of elders laid their hands on you.

As you consider Paul's instruction to Timothy, complete these sentences:

- I won't let anyone look down on me because _____.
- I will not neglect my gift, which _____.

SECTION ONE

A Purpose-Full Life

WORKING FROM THE HEART

Ruth Shaw is a marriage, family, and child counselor as well as a teacher of developmentally delayed three- and four-year-olds. One of Ruth's tasks is to assess children's delays and share that often painful information with parents. "Many have a sense that something is wrong and feel relieved to get a diagnosis. Others are in denial and don't want to hear the truth," says Ruth. "Their brokenness and disappointment break God's heart and mine. When parents comment that I have more compassion than other professionals they've dealt with, I know it comes from having a foster son with severe learning disabilities and a daughter with physical problems and learning disabilities. I've been on the parents' side of the table too."

Ruth's work as a therapist and teacher encompasses what she has come to see as her purpose in life: counting it a privilege to be present with people in their pain.

> A bruised reed he will not break,
>   and a smoldering wick he will not snuff out,
> till he leads justice to victory.
>   In his name the nations will put their hope.
>   (Matthew 12:20-21)

But Ruth expresses her purpose not only in her job, but throughout her everyday life. When her children bring friends home, they often end up talking with Ruth about their family problems. Says Ruth, "I am drawn to people who are hurting."

BEING AND DOING ARE INTERTWINED

Purpose in life is not just something we do. It involves who we are and our way of being in this world. Show Ruth Shaw hurting people, and she can't help but *be* with them. Living a purpose-full life involves both being and doing, which we often separate inappropriately and illustrate with stereotypes of Mary and Martha (Luke 10:38-42). Mary has been labeled the nonstop pray-er, and Martha the nonstop do-er. Women say, "I'm a Martha," to indicate they're active people and don't like waiting on God. Few women say, "I'm a Mary," because that would sound too holy. But according to these incorrectly pigeon-holed categories, the "Marys" are those of us who would rather pray for some-one than roll up our sleeves and help that person.

Even though purpose in life is about *doing,* it flows out of *being,* which is rooted in our relationship with God. Through daily interaction with God, we spot his purposes in Scripture and allow one, two, or several of them to arouse within us a curiosity, an extraordinary interest, and eventually a pas-sion for them. Our heart is broken by what breaks God's heart, and we devote our energies to those purposes. Our commitment to God's purposes influ-ences and changes our way of being a church member, parent, friend, grand-parent, or professional person.

Separating the inner spiritual life from outward purposes leads to frus-tration. If we detach these intertwined elements, we experience problems:

- DOING without BEING: If we serve others but don't sense God's daily companionship, we become do-gooders with nothing to sustain us and no source of integrity to guide us. It's easy to burn out or to develop an inflated sense of our own wonderfulness.
- BEING without DOING: If we have daily prayer and Bible study but don't allow our relationship with God to draw us into service, we come to know a me-centered God without knowing the God

who *so loves* the world. We become focused mostly on me, myself, and I.

These artificial categories have nothing to do with the way God wants us to live. Jesus set the example here on earth: He made frequent personal getaways to be with God (being), and he spent extravagant amounts of time introducing the kingdom of God by healing, teaching, and comforting others (doing). In the same way, our "devotional" moments and "service" moments are deeper opportunities to know God and partner with him in this world.

I believe Christians have learned to isolate these two aspects of life not from Scripture but from a culture that has stressed doing, but not being. This tragic separation has produced such havoc that even the secular women's movement is addressing the problem. Focusing on achievement alone isn't cutting it anymore. Women who have pushed through the glass ceiling of corporate management wonder, *Why isn't this as wonderful as I thought it would be?* Even a woman like Gloria Steinem, known worldwide for her life purpose of advancing the position of women, is now bringing up such topics as meaning in life and a proper souce of self-worth (both of which are spiritual issues) in her latest book, *Revolution from Within.* Without realizing it, many of us have followed her lead. We've done the "doing"; now it's time to explore the "being."[1]

Purpose in life involves both being and doing. In *How to Find Your Mission in Life,* author Richard Nelson Bolles states that it's impossible to discuss mission in life "without getting into religion." He points out that many leaders in the job-hunting field have been people of faith. What people need and want, he says, is this: "We want to marry our religious beliefs with our work, rather than leaving the two—our religion and our work—compartmentalized, as two areas of our life which never talk to each other. We want them to talk to each other and uplift each other."[2]

Bolles is correct, I believe. Any career search should involve examining the raw material God has given us in light of his eternal purposes (1 Corinthians 11:28; 2 Corinthians 4:18). For a job, vocation, or volunteer position to be full of meaning and purpose, it needs to draw on inner issues: values, beliefs, heartbreaks, relationship with God. Purpose in life is not just a matter of taking aptitude tests and classes; it is a spiritual quest in which we hunger to know what is in the heart of God for us to do.

PARTNERING WITH GOD

The key to linking our being and doing is to see our purposes in life as ways to join with God (being) in doing his will in the world (doing). A great help to me has been offering this prayer: "Let my heart be broken with the things that break the heart of God."[3] If we viewed life from God's viewpoint, what in this world would upset us? What upsets God that, if I'd let myself think about it, upsets me too? What needs to be changed? What needs more attention? What needs redemptive action? Where do God's pain and my pain intersect? Where do God's mystery and my purpose meet?

Finding our God-given purposes is much more than "getting lost in a cause bigger than ourselves." It's about developing a relationship with God in which we align ourselves so closely with him that his dreams become our dreams. His complaints become our complaints. His goals become our goals—even when our work appears unsuccessful or goes against what the church says is "business as usual." We become so attached to God we want to partner with him in redeeming people and situations, in expressing his joy, love, and creativity to the world. As we see what upsets God, it swells into personal frustration and compels us to ask, "God, how can you use me in this situation?"

Partnering with the Creator brings a divine satisfaction as God helps me feel in my bones the aches others feel in their bones. "The place God calls you to is the place where your deep gladness and the world's deep hunger meet," says Frederick Buechner.[4]

"The yearning to create—to generate, cultivate, restore, renew—lodges deep in the human heart," adds spirituality writer Jean Blomquist. "The seed of that yearning was planted at the dawn of creation, when God fashioned us in God's image, the image of the Creator. Our deep gladness characterizes the way, unique in each of us, that our yearning to create finds expression. The experience of deep gladness is a sign that we are living fully and fruitfully our God-given creativity. Perhaps that is why we feel so frustrated and unfulfilled when our work seems to inhibit rather than express our deep gladness."[5]

ROOTED IN A RELATIONSHIP

No matter what our purposes—whether impressive to others or hidden from them, requiring physical or mental stamina, new to us or a seasoned skill— they flow out of our primary reason for living: to know and love God. God created us to be in relationship with him, as pictured so well by his closeness to Adam and Eve, walking in the garden (Genesis 3:8).

Jesus clarified how the relationship with God takes priority over any religious activity: "To love him with all your heart, with all your understanding and with all your strength, and to love your neighbor as yourself is more important than all burnt offerings and sacrifices" (Mark 12:33). The Westminster Catechism states it well: "The chief end of man is to glorify God and enjoy him forever."

Meaning in life is not found in fulfilling divine purposes, but in a relationship with God. The apostle Paul didn't say, "For to me, to live is to preach to the Gentiles," but, "For to me, to live is Christ and to die is gain" (Philippians 1:21). Paul knew that dying would interrupt his purpose, but he still saw it as gain because his primary aim in life was to know Christ fully (Philippians 3:10).

This relationship with God then feeds our purposes in life without our fussing and straining too hard to discover or achieve them. The more fully we come to know God, the more clear his purposes become to us. The best way I know to illustrate this concept is to compare it to human relationships. For example, even though it's currently the rage to bash attorneys and make jokes about high fees, I was surprised one day to find myself defending attorneys. People around me stared as I explained how the court system requires an unprecedented burden, which results in excessive costs. The stares made me realize how much I had to say on the subject, and I wondered, *Where did this come from?*

One of my close friends, Barbara Gage, is the administrator of a large law firm, and through her I hear about the benevolent activities of the attorneys in her office and the challenges attorneys face. If anyone is qualified to bash attorneys, she is because she knows the worst. Instead she pleads their case. I spoke up in the discussion because someone I love has given me behind-the-scenes information. She has become very concerned that attorneys are regarded so poorly—and now, consequently, so am I.

In the same way, as we allow God to knit us to himself, his purposes rub off on us. (We'll look specifically at God's purposes in chapter 5.) Our love relationship with God makes us want to be a part of what he is doing. To be an onlooker would mean to be left out! What God says, feels, and does begins to set the framework for our decisions. Eventually, God's heartbeat becomes so loud that it's easier to join him than ignore his purposes.

BECOMING SINGLE-FOCUSED

But, you ask, *why narrow my focus to only a* few *purposes? Can't I find meaning in all sorts of things—kids' activities, church work, job opportunities?*

I have felt that frustration. The first time our family belonged to a large church, I sat in the sanctuary overwhelmed by all the activities and ministry opportunities listed on the back of the bulletin. I pointed to several and said to my husband, "Wouldn't it be great to do this…and this…and this?" For just a few minutes, I expected myself to be involved in everything in which I had the slightest interest. Others who knew me did too. "Do this—you're so good at this," or, "I can't believe you're not…"

If you are like me, you wonder if you should exclude yourself from activities not related to your specific purposes. After all, shouldn't Christians be concerned about all God's purposes? If a dynamic newsletter, a friend, or a church member appeals for my participation, shouldn't I volunteer? If I believe in pro-life issues, for example, how can I not be involved in all pro-life activities? Even with something as simple as Friends of the Library (our local library advocacy group), I feel guilty that I, a lover of books and an avid library user, have not joined.

Yes, all Christians should be concerned about all of God's purposes, but we can't all do everything that needs to be done. The church as a whole is Christ's body on earth, imitating Jesus Christ; he doesn't expect me to do it all myself. Once when I was overwhelmed with too many good ways to serve, a friend advised me, "You can't jump into every trench." Relieved to hear that, I had more energy to climb into the trenches I was sure God was calling me to abide in. We can't serve on the front lines of every purpose—giving significant time and energy—but we can support the purposes with which God breaks our heart. Not every need is a call from God.

In the classic book *A Testament of Devotion*, Quaker pastor and college professor Thomas Kelly talked about this: "But the Loving Presence does not burden us equally with all things, but considerately puts upon each of us just a few central tasks, as emphatic responsibilities. For each of us these special undertakings are our share in the joyous burdens of love....We cannot die on every cross, nor are we expected to."[6]

In a world of hurting people who need telephone calls and lawns mowed, it's difficult to tell what we're called to focus on. But when I know my specific purposes, I can better choose specific ways in which I will:

- serve in my church
- serve in my community
- donate money and leftover goods
- present needs to my children, nieces, nephews, and future grand-children
- know what books, magazines, conferences, and daily prayer guides I'll use so my heart can be broken on a regular basis with my purposes

But can't narrowing our focus preclude God's will? Yes, but that's where the *being* is so helpful. We miss what God wants us to *do* unless we have sought God for purpose and sensed his affirmation. Even then, we must continue to be open to the voice of God, eager to catch the details. People might criticize us for having a distinct focus as no doubt the apostle Paul was criticized for focusing on the Gentiles (Galatians 1:15-17). Paul was probably asked, *Aren't the Jews God's people? Aren't* you *a Jew?* But Paul heard God's call to go to the Gentiles and pursued it.

If sharpening your focus sounds too confining, consider the different ways a purpose can be fulfilled—researching it, teaching it, organizing it, presenting it to the church or community, giving money to it, gathering resources for it, raising funds for it, programming a computer for it, or cleaning up after all is said and done. God will help you use the aptitudes and skills with which he's gifted you to fulfill purposes that have broken your heart.

CLARIFYING WHO YOU ARE

One advantage of having our purpose in place is that we have a guideline for how to spend our time. Much has been said the last few years about overcommitment and learning to say no, but when we're thoroughly and fervently saying yes to God's purposes, saying no comes naturally.

For example, Henrietta Mears, longtime director of Christian education in Hollywood, California, spent her life finding better ways to disciple people, especially through teaching Scripture. Through her efforts to build a *better* Sunday school (she never tried to build a bigger one), the attendance increased from 450 to 4,200.[7] One of her specialties was teaching the church's college class, and there she discipled many future leaders of evangelicalism, including Bill Bright, founder of Campus Crusade, and the late Richard Halverson, longtime pastor and chaplain of the U.S. Senate.

When Fuller Theological Seminary was founded, Ms. Mears was asked to be the professor of Christian education. After she turned it down, she was admonished, "Your contribution to ministers would have been the acme of your educational career." Why did she refuse an opportunity to "expand" her ministry? "It is one thing to be a seminary professor and to instruct young men and women who have already committed themselves to the ministry; it is quite another to inspire university students who are trying to choose a life's calling. Miss Mears definitely had this latter gift," comments her biographer.[8]

Henrietta Mears's purposes were clear to her. She was drawn to an evangelistic edge of discipleship, bringing children off the streets to Sunday school and "doing personal work" with skeptical people who wanted no part of God. She loved debating with intelligent university students, watching them accept Christ, and then challenging them to ministry. While she served in Hollywood, more than four hundred college students turned their energies to preaching and missions.

Like Henrietta Mears, when we know our purpose, we can turn down opportunities graciously, saying, "I can see this is an important job, but it's not for me." We're no longer cornered by that phrase "but no one else will do it."

That doesn't mean we *never* volunteer in the nursery, help a friend in need, care for aging parents, clean up after a church potluck, or drive a carload of kids to summer camp. Those small acts of service enlarge our heart and remind us of our Savior in that difficult setting in which no servant was available to wash the guests' feet, and none of the group would budge—except Jesus Christ (John 13:1-17). In those moments in which no one seems willing to help, it just might be you or me who can help. But on an ongoing basis, we'll find it freeing to devote our energies to what we believe we have come to the kingdom for.

The apostle Paul tells us that we were created for a purpose: "For we are God's workmanship, created in Christ Jesus to do good works, which God prepared for us to do" (Ephesians 2:10). Our hunger for purpose was etched in our cells and bones and organs when we were made. Much of the dissatisfaction among Christian women today is, I believe, due to our choosing God as the center of our lives (being) but not linking up with the purposes God has put within us (doing). Full satisfaction will not come, of course, until we see Jesus face to face, but in the meantime we can enjoy a sense of fulfillment from interacting with God, both in being and doing.

QUESTIONS TO PONDER OR DISCUSS
Go to a quiet place, reflect on these questions, and don't feel hurried to come up with an answer. It may occur to you tomorrow or next week.
1. Why does what I do matter?
2. Who will profit? Who will be touched?
3. What could I do that *would* matter?
4. How is what I *do* linked to issues I can become passionate about?

EXPERIMENT IN LISTENING PRAYER
Lay these questions before God and see what comes to you in the silence and throughout the day:
* *What pulls at my heartstrings?*
* *What seems paramount in the midst of less important concerns?*
* *What makes me forget myself completely and be lost in a need?*

BIBLE PASSAGE TO CONTEMPLATE
Consider what God might be saying to you about your purposes through these verses:

> This is how we know what love is: Jesus Christ laid down his life for us. And we ought to lay down our lives for our brothers. If anyone has material possessions and sees his brother in need but has no pity on him, how can the love of God be in him? Dear children, let us not love with words or tongue but with actions and in truth. This then is how we know that we belong to the truth, and how we set our hearts at rest in his presence whenever our hearts condemn us. For God is greater than our hearts, and he knows everything. (1 John 3:16-20)

THREE

MISCONCEPTIONS ABOUT PURPOSE

I'll never forget the day I realized that my purpose in life was not to be a writer. I had been moving along as a published author in certain fields and had achieved a career high that excited me. But that day, as I left a convention center where a color photograph of me had been featured on translucent glass, I realized I felt empty. Since I was going on to a small town to meet up with an old friend, I headed for the bus station by transferring among four city buses. By the second one, I noticed I was the only white woman riding the bus. This was fine with me because this is what I'd been used to in urban ministry—a venue in which my husband and I had worked for fifteen years but which we had left feeling like failures.

I had more fun on those buses than I'd had for days—talking and joking within a diverse urban culture. When I arrived at the bus station, I sat down to talk with a woman who turned out to be a mother on public assistance. She told me her plan for getting off welfare and explained how, in the meantime, she was saving a few dollars from each check to buy children's classic books. What would I recommend? We had a delightful conversation.

As I walked over to the huge plate-glass window to watch the buses, I had a strong sense God was speaking to me about the purposes and direction of my writing. It wasn't enough to be a successful writer; I had to work with God in his purposes. At that moment, the voice on the loudspeaker announced that it was time for the prisoners to board my bus. *Prisoners?* I stared at the handcuffed juveniles, remembering what had always been my favorite Scripture: "I was hungry and you gave me something to eat… I needed clothes and you clothed me… I was in prison and you came to visit me" (Matthew 25:35-36).

What are you saying to me, God? I almost screamed aloud.

Back on the bus, I began to argue with God about my lifelong passion for social justice, especially racial reconciliation. I explained that I had been a failure in urban ministry. I reminded God how I'd written articles about these topics and had such difficulty selling them. Few magazines were interested in such things.

I kept pondering this conversation with God until a month later when I volunteered at the US Center for World Mission, where I heard a lot about God's covenant with Israel and how God blessed Israel so that Israel would bless all nations—not just to make Israel happy. I questioned whether I was using my blessings (my ability to make a living writing, which I loved) to bless others. I considered the articles and books I'd written on self-help issues and parenting. These had been good, but was this how I was created to bless others? Did these issues break my heart? Sort of…but they sold really well!

During my week at the center, my supervisor introduced me to many people, using the same wording each time: "She's written several recovery books and written for many magazines, including *Focus on the Family*." Upon hearing this introduction, one person eyed me closely and began quizzing me, "What are you recovering for? What are you focusing on the family for? What difference are you hoping to make for God and his kingdom?"

I darted out of there—fast—thinking, *This man has had too much coffee!* Sitting at my temporary desk once again, editing stories about peoples who had not yet heard the gospel, I asked myself, *What difference am I making? How am I advancing the kingdom of God?* That's when I came across a pamphlet with these words:

> Think over the energy you're throwing into life now—trying to
> be the best you can be, trying to get ahead, to be a better

Christian, a better family member, a better you. Why work so hard? Why ask so often for God's blessing on your life?

If it's to have a nicer, happier life, that's not a bad goal. Especially since that's what heaven will be—an easier, nicer existence. If that were God's purpose for you right now, He would simply take you home to heaven, right? But here and now, biblical discipleship is never described as "nice" or "easy."

God wants to bless you. But not to make your life easy. He'll bless you because He's got a demanding job for you—a specific task, one that lays down rails to guide your major life decisions, to keep you from *spinning your wheels in Christian self-improvement.*

Go ahead: Break out of the Christian-culture idea that to join God's family is to become part of a nice, privileged group. It's more like being born into a family business—everybody is naturally expected to take part in the Father's work.[1]

The phrase italicized above was also italicized in the pamphlet and it stood out. I had spent a lot of time "in Christian self-improvement," not spinning my wheels, but working out significant life issues. My ability to deal with life and other people was improving, and it was as if God, through the pamphlet, was asking me, *What will you do with these new skills and attitudes? I have blessed you; now how will you bless others? What is your role in "the Father's business"?* Had I been so concerned about achieving and doing that I had been afraid to seek God for my purposes in life? Writing was and still is the most exciting thing I've ever done, but what should I write about? How could I use writing to make a difference in this world? For years I'd believed in the importance of caring for people overseas by bringing them the gospel in word and deed, but I had done almost nothing about it.

I grabbed the brochure, put my head down on the desk, and admitted to God that my "career breakthroughs" were about me, not about the kingdom of God. To be honest, I had desperately wanted my life to be "nice and easy."

But on this day, my hour-long commute home was filled with these prayers:

- *Help me uncover the purposes I'm passionate about. I've buried them because they scare me.*
- *Help me become willing, God, to let you change the direction of my work.*

In the next weeks, months, and years, I made a lot of changes that terrified me. I journaled a great deal about the things that troubled me, and I began writing my list of purposes on a whiteboard above my desk:

- Out of my grief over the way Christianity tends to be so performance-focused, I found my first purpose: *communicating authentic spirituality.* That purpose is the topic of my retreat speaking. I've written books about knowing God intimately, led support groups at church with this emphasis, and tried to behave in the community groups to which I belong with this distinct focus in mind.

- Out of my grief over the poor and oppressed has come this purpose: *promoting social justice, especially racial reconciliation.* A few of the ways this purpose has taken shape are writing about topics related to world poverty, serving on the advisory board of a magazine for women of color, and volunteering at the Samaritan Center (a drop-in center for the homeless).

- Out of my frustration that the American church seems preoccupied with self-absorbed glitz has come this purpose: *focusing the American church on the substance of God's mission.* I'm currently working out this purpose through one of my retreat talks (linking purpose in life with authentic spirituality), writing magazine articles on these topics, reading *Global Prayer Digest* (almost) every day, and...writing this book.

- Out of my broken heart for pastor's families has come this purpose: *speaking to the unspoken hurts of pastors' families.* This purpose has resulted in writing articles related to this topic and speaking at pastors' wives retreats.

Today nearly all of my writing, speaking, and personal volunteering are related to these issues. I try to practice authentic spirituality in my parenting, and my kids have volunteered with me at the Samaritan Center enough to know the name of whoever might be standing on the street corner or hanging out in the public library bathroom. My magazine subscriptions revolve around these topics as do my memberships in organizations.

Can people have such divergent purposes in life? My experience would indicate so, although I don't see my purposes as diverse. To me, authenticity flavors the second, third, and fourth purposes, going back to my desire as a little girl to see the people at church go in to the bars and behave like Jesus.

One of the things that hindered me from understanding my purposes in life was the mistaken idea that purpose equals a job I love. I've discovered that our purpose in life can remain fuzzy or frustrate us when we link it specifically to concrete tasks and patterns. Jobs, roles, or working in a program may be specific ways to put our purposes into action, but they aren't life purposes. They don't grab our hearts and create an availability to God the way partnering with him does.

Let's look at some common misconceptions people have about purpose in life, both the things we mistake for purpose as well as the misguided belief that some people have a purpose and others don't.

Things Commonly Mistaken for a Life Purpose

A spiritual gift. Using your spiritual gift to organize a campaign, teach a class, or create a video presentation may intrigue you and even consume you because you're using the spiritual gifts God gave you, such as administration, teaching, or exhortation (see Romans 12:4-8; 1 Corinthians 12:1-13; Ephesians 4:7-13). Spiritual gifts aren't purposes, however, but helpful tools for doing tasks related to God's purposes. For me, writing (which some consider a vocation and others say is a spiritual gift) is my primary vehicle for expressing my purposes, but it is not my purpose in life.

Let's say you're an encourager—what are the causes, missions, and purposes for which you *must* provide encouragement or you will feel deep regret? Who are you unable to walk past on the street without offering a bit of hope? If your gift is teaching, what sort of person or circumstance breaks your heart? What topic are you being called to teach and to whom? If your gift is serving, where is the "place God calls you to [serve that] is the place where your deep gladness and the world's deep hunger meet"?[2] If it's giving, toward what purposes are you directing all that energetic reallocation of resources?

Discovering our spiritual gift isn't the same as discovering our purpose, but it's an important vehicle to help us fulfill our purpose and come to know God better.

A program you're devoted to. While programs such as Pioneer Girls and Bible Study Fellowship are excellent ways to work within our purpose, they are not purposes in themselves. If, however, we mistakenly view a program as our purpose, then we tend to work at making *that program* a success rather than following God's direction in fulfilling our purpose, which may be discipling girls or teaching truth. We even become calculating in our decisions and wonder about our contacts: *Will she support my program? Will he promote my work?*

In contrast, living a purpose-full life means we continually seek God about our role in any program, organization, or educational institution in which we serve, asking, "Is this part of how I'm to fulfill your purpose for me?" All that seeking enriches our relationship with God and informs us with nuances and wisdom regarding our purpose. We remain attached to God, not to the support group we started. When the group cannot continue or we move and can't participate anymore, we aren't devastated. We ask God to show us another avenue where we can use our passion for those who are hurting. If we mistakenly center our purpose in the support group, we will have lost our purpose in life, which isn't the way God works.

A person you're devoted to. Sometimes we get hooked on a person, such as a pastor, mentor, or boss. Without realizing it, we view our purpose as serving that person or becoming like that person. This person will fail us because he or she is human, and then we'll feel purposeless.

For example, Dana became the church secretary when an energetic, new pastor came to her church. She did her job well, grew close to the pastor, and played older sister to him. When he confessed to having had an affair and then left the church, Dana was devastated and quit her job. She figured there was no way God could use her now. The pastor was gone and the church would never be the same. It took her many years to see that God had called her to help people seeking God and she needed to find ways to keep doing that.

The only person to be devoted to is, of course, Jesus Christ. Within that relationship, we will find our purpose.

A role. Being a wife, mother, PTA president, or city council member is not a purpose in life. It's simply a role through which we may carry out our purposes. For example, some missionaries use that role to fulfill their purposes—penetrating specific cultural barriers with the gospel, caring for forgotten children, or making truth plain in accurate, readable translation work.

Yet people assume that if you have a specific role, you have recognized and are fulfilling your purpose in life. That's not necessarily so. For example, some missionaries aren't serving because they have a missions-related purpose, but out of a sense of guilt or duty or because they walked forward once as teen— or married a man who did.

A purpose in life must be much bigger than any role. Roles change because life circumstances change. For example, part of the lostness some women feel when their kids grow up and leave home is not only the companionship of their children but also their role of mothering, which became their purpose in life. When they "lost" their role, they lost their purpose. Others, however, learned their purpose through mothering; for example, they may feel called to speak up for those who cannot speak for themselves. When their children leave home, these women find ways to continue to fulfill these purposes.

Our purpose in life, when found in our relationship with God, remains the same even when our roles change. At age thirty, Christine Aroney-Sine joined Youth with a Mission's (YWAM) mercy ship, *Anastasis,* as the ship's doctor. She worked in that capacity for twelve years. Traveling to Third World countries to practice medicine, this single Australian woman became the chief medical officer for Mercy Ships International. When she developed chronic fatigue syndrome, she stayed with Mercy Ships International but had to leave duty on her ship. At the same time, she married and came to the United States.

Even with all these changes, Christine's purpose did not change: "I want to be a voice to the voiceless, to assist people at the bottom end of the ladder and be a spokesperson for those who are in some way excluded." On board the ship, she did this whenever they visited a developing nation. Now, she works as a consultant and lecturer on missions and international health for churches and mission organizations worldwide, including YWAM.

THE THINGS WE TELL OURSELVES...

Our misconceptions don't just lead us down the wrong path. Sometimes they allow us to "take ourselves off the hook" when it comes to identifying what our purpose in life might be. Perhaps you believe that some people have a life purpose, but not everyone is wired that way—including you. If so, you might be allowing one of the following thoughts to keep you from discovering your purpose.

I don't have a dynamic personality. Some women secretly believe, *Women who are energetic and outgoing have a mission in life. I just float along.* People with all kinds of temperaments can be purpose oriented, as biblical figures illustrate so well. The prophets Elijah and Elisha both yearned to bring Israel back into the arms of God, and both were passionate about speaking God's truth to the corrupt nation of Israel. But Elijah was an introverted loner, while Elisha spent a lot of time guiding a "company of prophets" (1 Kings 17:1-7; 2 Kings 2:3-7; 2 Kings 4–9). Elijah's miracles tended to be solo, dramatic achievements, while Elisha often helped large groups of people do practical things (1 Kings 17:8-24; 18:20-46; 2 Kings 2:19-22; 3:13-27; 4:38-44; 6:1-7). Both had passion and showed it in their own way—Elijah as a loner-style holy man and Elisha as a much-loved and respected mentor. Purpose is not tied to personality or style, but to an inner conviction of the heart.

Isn't passion a masculine thing? The fear behind this question is that a woman who pursues her purposes will become too aggressive, assertive, dominant, and decidedly unfeminine. But as the biblical, historical, and contemporary examples throughout this book show, passion for purpose was and is present in women through whom God works. (I discuss this more in the next chapter.)

We sometimes confuse cultural gender stereotypes with the commands of Scripture. Let's see how they compare. The first two columns in the chart below list cultural stereotypes, stated in extreme terms. Contrast these with the clear biblical mandates for both men and women in the right column.[3]

CULTURALLY "MASCULINE" PATTERNS (STATED IN EXTREME)	CULTURALLY "FEMININE" PATTERNS (STATED IN EXTREME)	BIBLICAL PATTERNS FOR MALES AND FEMALES
domineering	victimized	treating others with respect
angry	depressed	finding peace by processing anger and fear with God (consider the Psalms)
dictates	begs or schemes	cooperates with others as a team member
knows everything	knows nothing	has a wise, discerning, teachable spirit
arrogant	shut down, numb	attentive to others
out of touch with own feelings	overwhelmed by feelings	willing to express honest feelings to God (again, see the Psalms)
unwilling to show weakness	unwilling to show strength	confessing weakness to God and recognizing need for strength
ignores mistakes	makes excuses or obsesses about mistakes	admits failure and learns from it
feels superior	feels inferior	dies to self and focuses on others' needs, but finds worth in God's estimate of self

Many people equate energetic passion with the qualities in the first column, but biblically speaking, this isn't correct. As Christians seek God, the Holy Spirit does the work of transformation and the qualities in the last column appear. Energy, desire, and zeal are available to all, and these characteristics come, not laced with aggression and loudness, but empowered by God, who is eager to know us and love us as he accomplishes his work on earth through us.

It's true that risk taking is a characteristic of men in Scripture: Abraham packed up and went off to a strange land to pursue God's will; Moses fed and clothed a nation of people on the move, despite feelings of inadequacy; Nehemiah left the success and comforts of Persian palatial government to govern a ragtag outpost.

But women took risks as well. Consider Shiphrah and Puah, two Hebrew midwives who were called by God to facilitate birth but were told by Egyptian civil authorities to facilitate death. These women rose to the challenge, committed civil disobedience, and chose life for the baby boys (Exodus 1:15-21). In the New Testament, Mary dared to overspend a year's wages on burial perfume and make an exhibit of herself, anointing someone about to make the greatest sacrifice ever. She seemed to know about Jesus' death even though no one else was getting it (John 12:1-8). Mary, the mother of Jesus, dared to live in shame as an unwed mother, rearing a child who would be anything but predictable. As these examples show, God takes women on unpredictable paths of risk and provides the stamina to push through.

But I have to work. Sometimes employment is largely unrelated to our mission in life, but it can free us to have the time and income to fulfill our purposes. This was the experience of John Woolman, a New Jersey tailor and dry-goods-store owner in the 1700s. In the eternal scheme of things, this Quaker went from place to place preaching against slavery and making friends with Indians (although relations between them and the settlers were not peaceful).[4] His life purpose of peacemaking did not pay his bills, so he remained a tailor but kept his business small to allow more time for his preaching. Woolman's business financed his purpose, but his purpose also influenced his business. At one point, upon learning that the sugar and molasses he had previously sold in his dry-goods store were the fruit of West Indies slave labor, he took the profits from these items and purchased passage on a ship employed in the West India trade to "dissuade them from such unkind treatment." After Woolman did this, he also decided to boycott his personal use of molasses and sugar because of the "lamentable oppression" under which it was produced.[5]

But my job seems unspiritual. Perhaps the job that draws you seems downright antithetical to faith. If I'm fascinated by the earth and the way God created it, can I become a geologist—even though some consider all geologists to be antireligious evolutionists? Or, if I love the theater, but none of my fellow actors are churchgoers, what does that mean? Or, if the secret desire of my heart is to be a professional golfer, how can I be out on the course when others are at church on Sundays? It's important to investigate these desires to figure out if there's a purpose of God in them. Each of the three vocations mentioned above involve being salt and light to people who may not know Christ or aren't likely to attend church. Beyond that, these jobs hold many possibilities for purposes of God: to expose truth, such as the orderliness of God's creation (geology); to communicate attributes of God through fictional characters (theater); to experience and illustrate the rare combination of excellence and cooperation in a highly competitive situation (golfing).

If you believe God is leading you to pursue a certain profession, job, or hobby that seems unrelated to his purposes, learn about it and converse with God about what you learn. Ask God to speak to you about whether you could glorify him through that activity or whether you need to discard it. Understand that God worked through Nehemiah the politician, and he can work through you the stockbroker. God spoke through Amos the shepherd, and he can communicate through you the mobile pet groomer. God is, after all, the source of all knowledge, and all knowledge is his. The core issue is not whether the jobs involved in your purpose are populated by churchgoers, but whether you choose to know Christ and make him known in all your activities.

If you're currently in a job for which you can find no intrinsic purpose, consider the impact you make simply by being a person of good character. Anyone who doesn't sell out to greed or self-promotion and who isn't driven to be noticed or appear clever stands out from others. Ask yourself, *How can I align myself with God's purposes in this job? Which of those purposes am I passionate about?*

I'd hoped to be in the "Lord's work" but... In our culture, certain jobs are designated sacred and others secular. What makes a job the "Lord's work" is the purpose and heart of the person doing it, not the task itself. If I'm the historian for my church, it isn't the "Lord's work" when I am laced with perfectionism, focused on making a beautiful memory book but oblivious to God's people and purposes. It becomes the "Lord's work" when I use that scrapbook to document people's service in order to encourage others to have the heart of Christ. The kingdom is advanced when I use my abilities to welcome new Christians into the body of Christ or to celebrate the voiceless people who have been given a voice by our church.

Being a parent, accountant, respiratory therapist, researcher, secretary, grocery clerk, waitress, pilot, dentist, inventory controller, machine operator, or benefits administrator in a human resources department can be the "Lord's work" when we see ourselves as Christians whose primary purposes are to advance God's kingdom and promote reconciliation.

As we practice God's presence throughout the day—conversing with God about people, purposes, and techniques for getting things done—we'll discover that ways to advance the kingdom can be infused into every activity. For example, I write for magazines that are distinctively Christian and ones that are not. I can't imagine praying less for the editor of *Woman's Day* than I would for the editor of *Discipleship Journal.* Why would I? No matter who has hired me, I am God's child, aligned with him in the redemption of the world, listening to God about who he's calling me to be and what he's leading me to do.

A former archbishop of Canterbury, William Temple, once said, "It is a great mistake to think that God is chiefly interested in religion."[6] If not religion, then what? God is chiefly interested in people and their redemption.

If you found yourself within the pages of this chapter, I encourage you to ask God to show you the things you are passionate about and to help you be willing to let him change the direction of your work. If we are serious about being the women God created us to be, we must be willing to look into our hearts, even if there we find God's drawing us toward unlikely tasks that won't make sense to others.

QUESTIONS TO PONDER OR DISCUSS

Think back through the myths debunked in this chapter, then complete the following exercises:

1. Ask yourself, *When, if ever, have I substituted any of the following for purpose in life: a job I love, a program, a person, a role, a spiritual gift?*

2. Write a few paragraphs about what you would most like to do if time or money or skills or education weren't holding you back. Instead of being frustrated by the lack of resources to do this, lay it as a dream before God.

EXPERIMENT IN LISTENING PRAYER

Reread the indented quote near the beginning of the chapter ("Think over the energy you're pouring into your life..."), then ask God,

- *Have I been fooled into believing here-and-now, biblical discipleship is "nice" or "easy"?*
- *When in my life have I sensed I was part of God's "family business"?*

BIBLE PASSAGE TO CONTEMPLATE

> "For I know the plans I have for you," declares the LORD,
> "plans to prosper you and not to harm you, plans to give you
> hope and a future." (Jeremiah 29:11)

FOUR

THE FEMININE EDGE OF PURPOSE

As you reflect on the idea of purpose and what it may mean in your life, warning signals may be going off inside: *Put this book down! God doesn't use women like you.*

Most of us believe women can have purposes in life, but our belief remains a surface faith, not impacting the deeper levels of self. For example, is my belief that God uses women like me strong enough that I will ask a friend or spouse to pray for me about finding and pursuing my purpose? Do I believe in my purpose strongly enough to have the courage to do something about it? Do I believe firmly enough to set aside time to pursue it? Do I believe deeply enough to give up other things that distract me? Do I believe so fiercely that God has called me to a purpose-full life that I dare to be different from people around me?

Let me offer some reasons that continually help me to believe that women can and do have purposes in life, reasons that encourage me to keep on listening to God.

BIBLICAL WOMEN WHO PARTNERED WITH GOD

One idea that keeps women from pursuing their unique purposes is the myth that women are simply gap fillers for men—doing whatever men need done to fulfill God's purposes for their lives. This is based on the phrase in Scripture that speaks of God creating woman as a "help meet" or "helper" for man (Genesis 2:18, KJV, NIV). But does this word mean *gap filler, valet,* or *errand girl?* The root of this same Hebrew word is used elsewhere to describe God's role: "Do not hide your face from me, do not turn your servant away in anger; you have been my helper. Do not reject me or forsake me, O God my Savior" (Psalm 27:9; see also Psalm 10:14; Exodus 18:4). To say that women have no distinct purposes because of this "helper" description would be to imply that God is a gap filler, valet, or errand runner—which we would never say.

In addition, a lot of time has been devoted to the man-woman debate: What does "headship" mean? Can women be ordained? Those are important questions to study, but for our time together in this book, I encourage you to address two even more basic questions: Are women called to be servants of God? Are women, as well as men, given purposes from God?

Women of faith abound in the Bible, and God challenged them with divine purposes. I'll provide many scriptural examples throughout this book, but let's look at just a few now. The birth of Jesus was pre-announced both to the priest Zechariah, who didn't believe, and to the future mother, Mary, who did believe—and then rejoiced. It's true Jeremiah and Zephaniah wrote long books of prophecy, but Huldah was chosen instead of them to declare God's will for the people when the law was rediscovered in the temple (2 Kings 22:8-21; 2 Chronicles 34:14-28).[1]

An unnamed, apparently single woman (no mention is made of her father, husband, or brother, although most women were identified by such relationships in ancient Israel) talked back to a battering ram. King David's military commander, Joab, had built a ramp up to the city of Abel Beth Maacah and was battering the wall to bring it down. She confronted bloodthirsty Joab and appealed to his conscience: "We are the peaceful and faithful in Israel. You are trying to destroy a city that is a mother in Israel. Why do you want to swallow up the LORD's inheritance?" She found out what Joab wanted (the head of Sheba, a leader of the rebellion against David), discussed it with the townspeople, delivered the villain, and everyone went home (2 Samuel 20:16-22). Before you cross this woman off as unfeminine, consider her two outstanding characteristics—wisdom and peacemaking, two essential qualities for any well-functioning mother.

Even mothers in Scripture didn't limit their concern for well-being only to their families. For example, in the Old Testament, Hannah, who had wept bitterly over her infertility, rejoiced and sang when God gave her a child, viewing it as a great reversal for those who stumbled, for the poor and the needy (1 Samuel 2:4-8). Jesus' mother, Mary, saw the birth of Jesus as something bigger than her role as mother of the Messiah. She realized Jesus' birth was about God's working out justice and mercy in a land of tyranny. Mary recalled Hannah's song and also rejoiced in such reversals as God's filling the hungry with good things while sending the rich away empty (Luke 1:52-54). At the pinnacle moment of their lives, Hannah and Mary saw themselves as members of a global village. They looked beyond their own sphere to see how God used their blessing of childbirth to accomplish justice and mercy for others.

Both of these women also paid the severest price for partnering with God in redemption—they both gave up their sons. Hannah sent Samuel to live with the priest Eli in Shiloh, and Mary watched her son be executed. When Mary said, "I am the Lord's servant....May it be to me as you have said," she volunteered for a future in which "a sword [would] pierce" her soul (Luke 1:38; 2:35).

We can emulate Hannah and Mary today by viewing our struggles from a global perspective. Yes, it's often difficult to make ends meet, but my financial problems can prompt me to care more about a friend who is laid off. I can rub my tired feet at the end of a day, praying for the forty-five million adult women in developing countries who are stunted as a result of the malnourishment they suffered as children. I can wade through the boring aspects of my job or daily tasks and pray for the young girls in Latin America who work in garment factories for only thirty-eight cents an hour. I can celebrate my grade-school and high-school education by praying for the eighty-six million girls worldwide without access to schooling, and I can give money to help them receive some education.[2]

HISTORY SHOWS...

God has partnered with women for his divine purposes not only in Bible times, but also throughout history. American evangelical women through the years have significantly impacted the world, says Miriam Adeney, a wife, a mother of three teenagers, a cultural anthropologist, and a frequent contributor to *Christianity Today*. She notes that at the turn of the century three million American women were involved in more than forty women's mission societies. Thousands of women were serving as missionaries, and others were working in schools, hospitals, and colleges. The same women who were denied the right to vote throughout the 1700s and 1800s devoted their leadership skills to spearheading ministries to prostitutes, prisoners, and the poor.

Miriam describes one of her role models, Catherine Booth: "She had eight children. She wrote eight books. She had no word processor. She regularly went out and spoke to two or three thousand people a night in the slums. She had no Billy Graham Evangelistic Association to train counselors for her. She had to counsel them [herself]. And they were unemployed. They were, in fact, thieves and prostitutes. So she also had to do job training and placement for them. And yet, at the same time, she spoke to the wealthy."[3]

Miriam concludes: "Women would be much happier if we recovered the heritage that says, 'Attempt great things *for* God and expect great things *from* God.'"

Examples abound in both Scripture and modern history of women who have accomplished great things for God. A closer look often reveals that these women shared God's heart for redeeming vulnerable, hurting people.

In a speech at Radcliffe's commencement exercises in June 1993, Elizabeth Dole referred to this characteristic of purposeful women when she rephrased the question of Professor Henry Higgins in *My Fair Lady,* who asked, "Why can't a woman be more like a man?" Dole, former secretary of labor and now president of the American Red Cross, posed, "Why can't a woman be more like a woman?" and then quoted an article in *Life* magazine: "Women are more committed than men to cushioning the hard corners of the country, to making it a safer place. Women want stricter law enforcement against drunk driving and illegal firearms and drug dealing.…It's not that men don't care about these issues. It's simply that women care more."

"I don't know whether that's true," Elizabeth Dole commented on the article. "But perhaps our approach is different. Perhaps our involvement in public policy debates provides a leavening influence. Perhaps [having] more women in public service would result in a greater focus on cushioning corners for vulnerable Americans. If that's so, then it is doubly important that we women…rise to the challenge of leadership when we believe that to be our calling."[4]

Women—whether we be typists or doctors or roofers or home day-care operators—need to shed whatever holds us back from listening to God's distinctive call on our lives. And we need not be surprised if that call is somehow a " leavening influence" or "cushions corners for vulnerable" people.

WOMEN WHO DARE TO DREAM

In 1990 I was asked to tabulate and explain the results of a survey taken by *Virtue* (a magazine for Christian women) on the topic of women's dreams, including the ministries in which they'd like to be involved. I was inspired by the answers I read in the surveys, some of which I've listed below:

- teach a Bible study
- own a small farm for a retreat center
- lead children's music
- help abuse survivors
- fly a plane with Mission Aviation Fellowship
- go on a missions trip
- start an evangelistic choir of college and high school kids
- become a foster parent
- start a counseling center for abused women
- start a ministry to the homeless
- become a missionary
- get involved in creative, expressive sewing
- work with a deaf ministry
- house visitors

While some of these dreams may seem lofty, "one must think like a hero to behave like a merely decent human being."[5]

Besides, it's more dangerous not to dream. In a 1978 speech, Dr. Francis Schaeffer predicted the greatest threat to the cause of Jesus Christ as we approach the end of the twentieth century would be "if the United States became a nation filled with Christians whose goal in life is personal peace (or safety) and prosperity." Writers Bill and Kathy Peel observe, correctly I believe, his prediction is coming to pass:

> When safety and prosperity become our passions, we can be
> sure we've abandoned the pursuit of our God-given destiny in
> favor of a sub-standard life. If we were honest, we'd have to
> admit that this attitude is one of pure and simple fear. We don't
> take risks, we don't dream about doing great things because
> we're afraid that if we don't protect ourselves and our stuff, we'll
> lose what's ours—or what we *think* is ours. Ironically, we are
> never more vulnerable than when we are playing safe.[6]

A woman dabbling in God's purposes is certainly not playing it safe. She's looking into the heart of the God she loves and finding there a relationship to satisfy her soul and a purpose to stretch her heart.

VENTURING OUTSIDE TRADITIONAL WOMEN'S WORK

Sometimes, as in the case of the woman who wrote in the *Virtue* survey that she wanted to be a pilot for Missionary Aviation Fellowship, our dreams may point us to work that some view as masculine. As we saw earlier, God uses women for all sorts of tasks. We are mistaken to assume that his purposes for our lives must be linked to a traditionally female job or focus, such as the helping professions of medicine, education, mental health, or social work.

If you believe God has planted a desire within you and has given you aptitudes to accomplish it, explore how that desire can be used to advance his kingdom. That's what Evelyn Curtiss did.

As a young African-American woman, Evelyn had a head for business and a heart for God. Business courses attracted her, but she wondered if God could use a woman in this traditionally male role. As she heard Proverbs 31 taught one day, she saw in that passage a businesswoman who advanced the kingdom of God.

"I had a strong desire in my heart to be used in practical ways in business and ministry," says Mrs. Curtiss, now in her sixties. "In the Proverbs 31 woman, I saw my life goals, desires, and dreams: a woman who loves God, is a good wife, a good manager of her home, a businesswoman, a woman concerned about her community. I studied that passage and prayed about it."

Through her careful management of a bookstore in south-central Los Angeles, Evelyn Curtiss (with her husband, Rev. Joe Curtiss of United Gospel Outreach) has advanced the kingdom in her community. "We hire young people, give them their first jobs, and teach them appropriate job conduct. Young people who have started here have gone on to Bible college or become nurses and teachers. Because we hire kids in the community, it's given us a relationship with children in the community.

"The bookstore has also been a steppingstone to ministry. We've provided economic development in the form of jobs, job training, and income for families. The bookstore's income has funded outreach programs and provided supplemental income for me as a missionary with American Missionary Fellowship. It has also been an avenue for teaching inner-city pastors and churches by providing workshops and conferences for ministry to youth, children, and adults."

People have advised Evelyn and her husband to take their children and move out of south-central Los Angeles. "We live in the Seventy-seventh Precinct, which has the highest crime rate in the city of L.A.," she says. "The economic level is extremely low with high unemployment, drugs, crack houses, poverty, crime, struggling businesses, and shattered families. For thirty-six years, the bookstore, alongside the United Gospel Outreach building, has stood out as an oasis. We give the business a clean, first-class appearance, not a junky, half-run look. We're saying, 'This is how it should be and can be.'"

So what purpose is being fulfilled by this dashingly feminine woman? Evelyn Curtiss has used her love of business and books to be a provider of resources in a neighborhood desperate for resources. Out of that business have come not only books but also classes, jobs, job training, and economic development. She has not only handed out a "cup of cold water" or two; she is equipping people to go to the well and draw water for themselves (Matthew 10:42).

THE HEART OF THE MATTER

When it comes to using someone for his purposes, God seems to be more concerned about character than he is about gender or circumstances. The biblical character Abigail is a good example of this. She understood God's purposes of mercy, justice, reconciliation, and advancing the kingdom, and she acted within them even in complicated circumstances. Her husband, Nabal, was rich and powerful, but he was neither compassionate nor just. When David and his men asked for food in return for helping Nabal's shepherds, he refused to comply with this common practice. Instead, he insulted David, who planned to attack him in revenge.

As Nabal's wife, Abigail had access to incredible resources—enough to gather quickly two hundred loaves of bread, meat from five sheep, a sack of roasted grain, and hundreds of handfuls of raisins and figs (1 Samuel 25:18, CEV). She sent these resources to David, preventing a skirmish that would have left many dead. When she spoke to David, kingdom values laced her speech. She rescued David's conscience from a ruinous, barbaric decision, reminding him of his royal purpose and integrity so that when he became king he would "not have on his conscience the staggering burden of needless bloodshed" (1 Samuel 25:31). Abigail's big-picture thinking—respect for God instead of petty revenge against either David or Nabal—reflected God's will. By aligning herself with God's purposes, Abigail found the positive edge of peace, reconciliation, and generosity, and she behaved in a redemptive way.

And she did this with such class. She showed how it's possible to resolve unjust situations with compassion and graciousness. She didn't cringe and grovel before David; she spoke to her future king boldly but respectfully, appealing to his integrity. Abigail's sensible, caring approach in the midst of Nabal and David's frenzied disagreement saved the lives of many and must have been impressive. No wonder David accepted her offer and later asked her to marry him (1 Samuel 25:2-44)!

Abigail's heart was so aligned with God's that she could be used when her husband could not. She saved men's lives, as well as her future king's conscience, because she did not accept the myth that a woman like her couldn't possibly have any influence. By abandoning that myth, we, too, can be ready to be used for God's purposes.

WHAT HAVE YOU COME TO THE KINGDOM FOR?

Whether because of our culture, our upbringing, or our skewed interpretations of Scripture, we women are often too limited in our thinking about the difference we can make in this world. Miriam Adeney, who is also a professor at Seattle Pacific University and Regent College, challenges herself and other women with the purpose-driven question Mordecai asked Esther, *What have you come to the kingdom for?*[7] "Working for the kingdom means expressing, reiterating, claiming, insisting on [God's] reign for our homes and neighborhoods all the way up through our country's international relations," writes Adeney in her book, *A Time for Risking*. "Given this high-level job, how small are our ambitions. How trivial are our pursuits. What have we come to the kingdom for? Shopping malls? Food processors? Home computers? Luncheons? The command is to seek first the kingdom."[8]

Her point is well taken. I've noticed that the most frequent topic of conversation among Christian women seems to be purchases, sales, and bargains. Have we succumbed to the cultural theme, "I shop, therefore I am"? Although spiritual writer Evelyn Underhill lived long before the megamall era, she wrote, "We mostly spend those lives conjugating three verbs: to *want*, to *have*, and to *do*. Craving, clutching, and fussing on the material, political, social, emotional, intellectual, even on the religious plane, we are kept in perpetual unrest."[9]

As women in search of purpose, let's take up a different agenda, one that flames up from a burning heart for the kingdom of God. May we "pursue the things over which Christ presides. Don't shuffle along, eyes to the ground, absorbed with the things right in front of you. Look up, and be alert to what is going on around Christ—that's where the action is. See things from *his* perspective" (Colossians 3:2, *The Message*).

QUESTIONS TO PONDER OR DISCUSS

1. What fears, if any, affect your beliefs regarding a woman having purposes in life?
2. When have you seen women provide a "leavening influence, cushioning the corners for vulnerable" people?
3. What secret dreams have you never told anyone about?

EXPERIMENT IN LISTENING PRAYER

Ask God, *What, if anything, about myself as a woman holds me back from pursuing purposes in life?*

BIBLE PASSAGE TO CONTEMPLATE

The Proverbs 31 passage describing a virtuous woman made an impression on Evelyn Curtiss, while other women feel intimidated by the description of a woman who can juggle so much. Reread this passage and quietly contemplate verses 8-31. Wait to see which phrase from these verses stands out to you. Then bring that to God in prayer and see if there's anything about that phrase that God may be using to speak to you about your purpose.

FIVE

LINKING UP
WITH GOD'S PURPOSES

At this point you may be hoping that I've included an index in the back of the book that lists, say, the top ten purposes in life, and that you can take a simple test to figure out which one is yours. Then below that quiz is a list of six tasks you can choose from to fulfill your purpose. That done, you'll live happily ever after, right?

But this is not how purpose works. Because purpose flows out of our relationship with God, our purposes are part of our spiritual journey. Our understanding of purpose will grow as our relationship with God matures. As God leads us into a life of greater trust, integrity, and selflessness, doors will open and we'll be equipped for tasks that once scared us. In our conversations with God, we will find courage to experiment with different purposes and this will refine our mission.

THE HEART OF GOD

Our hearts can't be broken with the things that break God's heart unless we're aware of his purposes in this world as made clear in the broad themes of Scripture. Let's look at the kinds of things Scripture records God doing and link them with a specific purpose.

In the Old Testament, we see God:

- *creating beauty that shouts of his presence.* God made the earth in its "vast array." This creation was good, full of God's love, and praised God (Genesis 1–2:1; Psalm 33:5-6; 69:34).

- *making truth plain.* God gave explicit laws printed by his own finger on stone tablets (Exodus 31:18; Deuteronomy 4:13). He offered proof of his promises to Gideon through miraculously wet and dry fleeces (Judges 6:14-40).
- *offering freeing truth about what keeps our bodies healthy.* God communicated guidelines for health and hygiene (Leviticus 11–15).
- *freeing the captives.* God delivered the Hebrew slaves from Egypt and brought them to the Promised Land (Exodus, Numbers, Deuteronomy). He brought Judah out of captivity, back to the homeland (Ezra, Nehemiah).
- *providing avenues of justice in society.* God offered guidelines of what to do when someone caused a death (Numbers 35). He insisted on fair commerce and business practices (Leviticus 19:35-36).
- *prescribing merciful methods for caring for the poor.* God used the year of Jubilee to cancel debt, check slavery, and prevent people from securing unfair advantages (Leviticus 25:8-55; 27:17-24). He required landowners to leave enough crops unharvested to be gleaned by the poor (Leviticus 19:9-10).
- *binding up the brokenhearted.* God (through Elijah) raised from the dead the only son of the widow of Zarephath (1 Kings 17:9-24).
- *forging lasting covenants.* God initiated a covenant with Abraham (Genesis 17:5-14). He used a rainbow as a covenant that he would never again destroy all life by flood (Genesis 9:12-17).
- *welcoming strangers and aliens.* God warned Israel not to mistreat immigrants, but to welcome them (Leviticus 19:33-34).
- *offering help to the person or nation in trouble.* God spoke kindly to Hagar (partly victim, partly culprit) and spared her life and her son's life (Genesis 16; 21:8-21; see chapter 9 of this book). God spoke through Old Testament prophets to draw Israel back to him and away from idols (Isaiah–Malachi).

In the New Testament, we see Jesus:

- *communicating God's truth in such a way that hearts burn.* Jesus talked with the disciples on the road to Emmaus so that their hearts burned (Luke 24:13-35).
- *meeting the needs of the sick.* Jesus healed Peter's mother-in-law (Matthew 8:14-17). He restored the withered arm of a man (Mark 3:1-6).
- *spending time with outcasts.* Jesus talked with and cast the demons out of the local "crazy person" who lived in the cemetery, naked and alone with his demons (Luke 8:26-39). Jesus frequently healed lepers, equivalent to the AIDS patients of his day (Mark 1:40-45).
- *providing joyful celebrations.* Jesus saved the wedding feast at Cana from being ruined by turning water into extra wine (John 2:1-11).
- *exposing truth through humor.* Jesus compared the hypocrisy of the Pharisees to odd behaviors (Matthew 23:23-32). He compared the rigidity of the Pharisees to exploding containers of wine (Luke 5:30-39).
- *helping people see truths about the heart of God through stories.* Jesus told parables such as the merciful Samaritan and the prodigal son (Luke 10:25-37; 15:11-24).
- *showing concern for people of all nations to the point of shocking his Jewish followers.* Jesus cast the demon out of the daughter of the Canaanite woman (Matthew 15:21-28). After healing the servant of the Roman centurion, Jesus commended him for his great faith (Matthew 8:5-13).
- *creating safety for people to tell the truth.* Jesus healed the hemorrhaging woman and enabled her to tell the "whole truth" about herself (Mark 5:21-34).
- *feeding the hungry.* Jesus fed many crowds numbering in the thousands (Matthew 14:13-21; 15:29-38).
- *loving and caring about children.* Jesus made time for children and showed concern for their welfare by blessing them (Matthew 19:13-15).
- *confronting people in their sin.* Jesus asked the rich young ruler to give up his riches (Mark 10:17-25).
- *challenging people to move beyond their limitations and thought processes.*

Jesus asked the thirty-eight-year invalid if he wanted to walk (John 5:1-9). He urged the seeking Pharisee, Nicodemus, to be born again (John 3:1-21).

- *caring for caregivers.* Jesus not only cast a demon out of a boy, but talked with the father (Mark 9:14-27).

Woven throughout these examples is the big-picture theme of redemption. Each passage points to God's desire to connect with humankind and establish a love relationship with us. It began in the Garden of Eden where God walked with Adam and Eve. After the breach of the Fall, God began this business of redeeming us as his own again. Christ himself is called the Redeemer seventeen times, and the words *redeem, redeemer,* and *redemption* occur in Scripture more than one hundred times in references such as these:

> And who is like your people Israel—the one nation on earth
> that God went out to *redeem* as a people for himself, and to
> make a name for himself, and to perform great and awesome
> wonders by driving out nations and their gods from before
> your people, whom you *redeemed* from Egypt? (2 Samuel 7:23,
> emphasis added)

> Jesus Christ, who gave himself for us to *redeem* us from all
> wickedness and to purify for himself a people that are his very
> own. (Titus 2:13-14, emphasis added)

Look again at the first Old Testament example of God's fulfilling his purposes and notice how redemption moves out from the heart of God into his behaviors. In the first example, God's work was not only a beautiful creative act, but it also provided constant evidence to lost humankind that God created us. (In Romans 1:20, Paul offered creation as evidence for the existence of God.) This evidence helps people agree to be redeemed. In the New Testament list, the first example shows Jesus' communicating truth in a such a powerful way that the disciples' hearts "burned." He did this to reconcile those disciples' despairing hearts to the Savior they saw crucified and raised, to give direction to men who weren't sure what would happen next. Everything points to redemption, and our specific purposes in life are somehow related to partnering with God to redeem the world.

REDEMPTIVE BEHAVIOR—WHO ME?

But the idea of redemptive behavior isn't a familiar one. Even *thinking* redemptively is a challenge! The first time I remember being asked to think redemptively, it confused me. An editor wanted me to write a magazine article about how parents of teens can help their kids deal with violent situations. The editor, a Christian, explained she didn't want me to tell parents how to protect their kids from violent situations at school and the neighborhood. "Speak to the topic redemptively," she told me. *What does that mean?* I wondered, but I didn't ask because I didn't want to sound dumb.

This editor went on to talk about what teens could do or be to turn a violent person or situation around. I was stunned. Teenagers acting as peacemakers? That scriptural phrase "he has committed to us the message of reconciliation" (2 Corinthians 5:19) couldn't apply to my teenagers, could it? For most of my adult life, I'd lived in a high crime area of Los Angeles. Would I ask my precious teenagers to be redemptive? I was so challenged by the idea that I couldn't bring myself to think about it.

For my article, I managed to find someone else's teenager who behaved redemptively in a violent situation, breaking up a racial disturbance in a high school. Still stunned, I brought this up at the dinner table with my family. As we talked, I remembered how I had broken up a fight on a south-central Los Angeles playground at my kids' elementary school. True, I'd put them in the car first, but they saw what I did. I didn't mention this to my teens that night at dinner because I was afraid they might go out and do some foolish, redemptive thing! But I began praying for the strength even to *want* my kids to behave redemptively rather than choosing the softer, easier path in life.

Through this experience, I saw redemptive behavior in a way I'd never seen it before. Any time we cooperate with God in "buying back" people from their slide into despair and sin, we behave redemptively. One of the most powerful moments in Victor Hugo's *Les Misérables* comes after the bishop, Monseigneur Bienvenu, keeps the main character, Jean Valjean, from returning to prison by telling the police that the items Valjean had stolen from his home were gifts. In response to Valjean's confusion, Monseigneur Bienvenu says, "It is your soul that I am buying for you. I withdraw it from dark thoughts and…I give it to God!"[1] After that incident, Valjean not only becomes scrupulously honest and industrious; he participates redemptively in the lives of others.

Are we asked to be as radical as the bishop? Yes, but redemptive behavior takes different shapes and sizes, depending on God's call in your life. For example, if you want to start a Bible study, a particularly redemptive way to do so would be to target a group of people who are likely to slide into despair. That's what Dr. Katherine Bushnell (1856–1946) did. When she wasn't serving as a missionary in China, she walked from door to door in America inviting desperately needy women to prayer meetings in attractively furnished, free reading rooms. She began securing employment for many of them and outlined a plan for expanding that work throughout the city and the nation. During this period she also founded the Anchorage Mission for homeless women in Chicago, where as many as five thousand women found shelter in a single year.[2] Katherine Bushnell intervened in the lives of women who lived without hope and who might otherwise never have known Christ. Her intervention was a redemptive act.

Or consider a contemporary woman, Elaine Barsness, who with her husband, Gary, has parented nearly ninety foster children, giving these children security and focused care while their parents regroup. Several of these children have been drug babies who cry constantly. At first, this redemptive work was scary for Elaine. "Since you didn't know the kids, it was like marrying someone without meeting them," she says. "It was also hard because we were pretty social. All of a sudden, we had extra kids—nine- and ten-year-old boys. People didn't want to invite us over as much. They worried that our boys would steal from them or abuse their kids. We got used to being left out and spent more time with our family."

Another example of a redemptive task is the one I see increasing numbers of women becoming trained to do: acting as a court-appointed child advocate. These servants listen to a child embroiled in a legal matter, such as a custody dispute, and then speak to the judge from the child's viewpoint. This unpaid, volunteer activity buys back a child's ability to speak to the most powerful person in his or her life.

Redemptive work costs us, but it's well-spent energy. "You definitely have to die to yourself," says Elaine. "Somebody cries in the middle of the night and needs a bottle, so you get up whether you want to or not. Things get on your nerves. I have to ask God to give me strength.

"I don't feel like I'm a talented person who can deal with children, using clever discipline techniques," she continues. "I'm just a mom willing to do the mom thing with one more kid." But Elaine's enthusiasm is contagious; six couples she knows have become foster parents.

FLESHING OUT REDEMPTIVE PURPOSES

God invites us to join his redemptive, "family business"-style efforts to buy back people, to make them one with him again, to restore and liberate people—ourselves included—from desolation, human wickedness, and isolation from God. There are many ways to behave redemptively and to describe them would require a separate book, so let me offer a few of the ones I see in Scripture:

God's redemptive purposes include reconciling the world to himself and reconciling people to each other. God's purpose behind the life and cross of Christ is to reconcile humankind to himself. For example, Jesus appalled the disciples by standing in a public place in broad daylight, discussing morality and spirituality with a pagan Samaritan woman (John 4:4-28). Later he stood in another public place and drew a woman out through conversation until she told him the "whole truth," possibly even speaking of an unspeakable woman's disease she'd had for twelve years (Mark 5:24-34). In still another public conversation with another pagan woman, Jesus sparred verbally with the her passionate pleas and finally complimented the woman on her faith and healed her daughter (Matthew 15:21-28). Normally, pagans were shunned and women were disregarded; no wonder the disciples were so confused by this Savior who looked at status upside down.

Jesus didn't do these things to shock people, but because "I do nothing on my own but speak just what the Father has taught me" (John 8:28). As God on earth, Jesus behaved with justice and mercy, discernment and redemption, truth and wisdom. Christ's way of living challenges us to replace radically the typical overriding questions of life with his concerns. Instead of asking ourselves, *What can I do to make my life more comfortable?* we ask, *What can I do to know Christ and align myself with his work in the world?*

Two women who seemed eager to partner with Christ and forsake being comfortable were Angelina and Sarah Grimke. These two Southern women in the 1800s were daughters of a wealthy slave owner, but because they listened to the heart of God they became active in the abolitionist movement. These two single women went on a nine-month speaking tour in seventy towns where they were jeered and attacked. When Angelina spoke to the Massachusetts state legislature regarding abolition, she was the first woman ever to address this assembly.[3] Instead of being preoccupied with their wealth, status, and upbringing, these two sisters participated in what they believed was God's redemptive work.

Redemption is about reconciling people to God and to others and even to their own true selves:

> All this is from God, who reconciled us to himself through Christ and gave us the ministry of reconciliation: that God was *reconciling* the world to himself in Christ, not counting men's sins against them. And he has committed to us the message of *reconciliation*. We are therefore Christ's ambassadors, as though God were making his appeal through us.
> (2 Corinthians 5:18-20, emphasis added)

Reconciliation plays itself out in many different tasks: loving and counseling a burned-out Christian; taking a teenager into your home; nurturing weary pastors' families; helping senior citizens find peace with the God who is waiting to welcome them; introducing peoples of the Eastern Hemisphere to the original Eastern religion of Jehovah God and his Son, Jesus Christ; or as a child sponsor, showing love to one small girl in Honduras with Bible classes, friendship, one square meal every day, and the opportunity to go to school. Reconciliation is *redemptive* because it imitates the ultimate redeeming act of Christ, who lifted the curse from us and freed us to find peace with God (Galatians 3:13-14).

God's redemptive purposes include advancing his kingdom. Jesus came to usher in the kingdom of God ("the kingdom" is mentioned more than one hundred times in the Gospels alone), and God reconciles himself to us through that kingdom. Jesus stated that, as a member of God's family, "the kingdom of God is within you" (Luke 17:21), which was quite a stunning statement. So it is now our business to "advance" that kingdom: "From the days of John the Baptist until now, the kingdom of heaven has been forcefully advancing, and forceful men lay hold of it" (Matthew 11:12). Jesus' famous "last words" entrusted us with this purpose: Go, make disciples of all nations, baptize them into the family, guide them in ways of obedience (Matthew 28:19-20). Whenever we make known the mind and heart of Christ—through mentoring, teaching, caring, evangelizing, and so on—we are advancing the kingdom.

The command to advance the kingdom to "all nations" (this phrase occurs thirty-five times) is sometimes falsely interpreted to mean only one thing: becoming a missionary. While this is a magnificent way to advance the kingdom, there are many ways to pay attention to how God is working to redeem other cultures. Many Christians visit university campuses and offer English tutoring to the thousands of international students in this country, caring for their needs and eventually introducing them to Christ. Other Christians go out of their way to cross cultures in their neighborhood or reach out to Hindu, Buddhist, or Muslim coworkers. Still others partner closely with missionaries abroad by acting as forwarding agents and intercessors for unreached peoples.

When I volunteered at the US Center for World Mission, the missionaries assigned there talked about the underestimated importance of prayer and encouraged me to keep praying daily for unreached people. I've done this for more than ten years now—with the guidance of *Global Prayer Digest*[4]— and it has changed the way I view the world's nations, opening my eyes to the work of God around the world. Many times when I've been wrapped up in petty worries, I read *GPD* and come away with a larger perspective of reality. Being conscious of advancing God's kingdom worldwide binds us more closely to the heart of God, who loves all people and calls us to do the same.

God's redemptive purposes include providing a voice for the voiceless. Many of the people Jesus reached out to were people who had no voice in their own culture. They were sick, outcasts, Gentiles, children, or widows. He came to provide for them what no one else could: justice, mercy, and faithfulness. This trio of traits, overlooked by the Pharisees, are precisely the ones Micah implored corrupt Judah and Israel to recover: "But you have neglected the more important matters of the law—*justice, mercy and faithfulness*" (Matthew 23:23, emphasis added). "He has showed you, O man, what is good. And what does the LORD require of you? To *act justly* and to *love mercy* and to *walk humbly with your God*" (Micah 6:8, emphasis added).

These three traits reflect the personality of God himself, who is fair but merciful, just yet loving, and always steadfastly faithful. When we show mercy, justice, and faithfulness to those in our culture with no voice, we are partnering with God in redemption.

Professor of philosophy and ordained minister Dallas Willard says that "possibly *the* most pervasive theme of the biblical writings" is the "transformation of status for the lowly, the humanly hopeless, as they experience the hand of God reaching into their situation."[5] How can we show concern for the lowly as Hannah and Mary did? Dallas Willard helps us by naming for us those who are seriously crushed today:

> The flunk-outs and drop-outs and burned-outs. The broke and
> the broken. The drug heads and the divorced. The HIV-posi-
> tive and herpes-ridden. The brain-damaged, the incurably ill.
> The barren and the pregnant too-many-times or at the wrong
> time. The overemployed, underemployed, the unemployed.

The unemployable. The swindled, the shoved aside, the
replaced. The parents with children living on the street, the
children with parents not dying in the "rest" home. The lonely,
the incompetent, the stupid. The emotionally starved or dead.[6]

What all these people have in common is that they are voiceless in some
way. God calls his people to be a voice for the voiceless, as Jesus reached out
to those who were voiceless in his local Jewish culture: children, women, non-
Jews, anyone who was poor or sick, those who had lost limbs or were pos-
sessed with a demon. In our day, it's not much different. Healthy people
easily forget those who are tucked away with an infirmity.

How can I be a "helper" to a voiceless person—a Down syndrome child,
a Vietnam veteran with post-traumatic stress disorder, a child in the Third
World who is dying because her parents don't have the ten dollars for a doctor and transportation to travel twenty miles to the nearest hospital? Simply
as a citizen of the richest nation of the world, I am a person with a voice and
I can express my opinion and vote regarding decisions about trade, ecology,
and foreign diplomacy—all of which can mean plenty or poverty to a family
in the Third World. In conversations where any category of voiceless people
come up, I can bring up ideas others may not have considered.

But my normal human nature wants me to spend my energies being my
own advocate. I want to argue for more tax money to my neighborhood,
not a poorer one across town. I want to have a servant's heart, but often I don't.
Dallas Willard expresses a similar uneasiness:

> Can't we feel some sympathy for Jesus' contemporaries, who
> huffed at him: "This man is cordial to sinners, and even eats
> with them!" Sometimes I feel I don't really want the kingdom to
> be open to such people. But it is. That is the heart of God. And,
> as Jonah learned from his experience preaching to those wretched
> Ninevites, we can't shrink [God's heart] down to our size.[7]

As we fulfill our God-imbued purposes, God seems to use them to teach
us the character we're lacking. As I've read about and become more concerned

about voiceless people, I've come to see that voice-giving is not an outward behavior only, but a burning passion that flows from our relationship with God. As my heart is broken for how hungry children in Third World nations can't afford even a tetanus shot, I become more attentive to the sometimes obnoxious little girl on my street who has used deviant behavior to get my attention. I've come to see she is a voiceless person in her world, and so I try to remember to stop and give her my full-faced attention when I see her. Being mindful of God's purposes is not devotion to a cause but a *way to be in this world.*

Our God-given purposes in life flow from our hearts and relate in some way to this theme of redemption, whether they reflect reconciliation or advancement of the kingdom of God or being a voice to voiceless people. In the next section, we'll look at discovering our purposes in life, but in a sense we begin here. The prayer, "Let my heart be broken by the things that break the heart of God" assumes we are seeking the heart of God. May this chapter move you farther down that road of seeking God's heart.

QUESTIONS TO PONDER OR DISCUSS

1. What examples of redemptive behavior can you recall seeing in others—ways in which someone bought another person back from a desperate situation?

2. Which of these themes speak to you in a most personal way? Why?
   - reconciling the world to God
   - reconciling people to each other
   - advancing the kingdom of God
   - being a voice for the voiceless

EXPERIMENT IN LISTENING PRAYER

Ask God, *Open my eyes to the things that break your heart.*

BIBLE PASSAGE TO CONTEMPLATE

Read the gospel of Mark or at least chapters 1–8. What fascinates you about Jesus? What was he trying to accomplish in people's lives?

Now think back to your favorite stories from the Old Testament. Look up several and ponder: What kind of work was God doing in those stories?

Uncovering Your Purposes

LOOKING FOR CLUES

As a young adult, Mary Phillips married Bob and became the instant mother of his daughter. This was not the age of blended families, and Mary had no self-help books to show her how to redeem their daughter from the despair of her mother's death or how to persuade the child to allow Mary into her life. Through trial and error Mary found that telling her new daughter something didn't work as well as asking questions and listening to find out what she needed. Over the years the family melded. Eventually Mary and Bob had two more children, and she operated the same way with them.

As these kids grew up, Mary became a successful real estate agent, but she didn't take the path most agents use to build a business—listing as many homes as they can. Mary did the opposite. She found clients who needed homes (and they found her), and then she studied the listings to help them out. Quite often, clients bought the first home she showed them because of her precise research and ability to hear what they wanted in a home.

Now in her sixties, Mary finds her appointment book filled with women who want to be mentored. She looks back and sees that in every meaningful experience of her life, she has helped people find a sense of home and belonging, whether they be children, clients, or younger women. Providing a sense of home is a familiar theme to God: "If anyone loves me, he will obey my teaching. My Father will love him, and we will come to him and make our home with him" (John 14:23). As Mary aligned herself with God, this red thread of purpose wove itself through her life.

As with Mary Phillips, the duties and roles we have chosen can provide us with clues about our God-given purposes. So if you're thinking, *I'd love to have a purpose in life—but I don't know what it is,* take heart. Your purpose resides within you. In the next few chapters, we'll look at four phases in discovering our purposes, which are based on the four stages of creativity (popularized by many authors, including Ernest Rossi and Milton Erickson[1]) that often parallel other kinds of inward growth:

- Phase 1: Data collection—gathering what you need to know (this chapter)
- Phase 2: Incubation—mulling it over (chapter 7)
- Phase 3: Illumination—experiencing breakthrough (chapter 7)
- Phase 4: Verification—receiving feedback (chapter 7)

PHASE 1: DATA COLLECTION—GATHERING WHAT YOU NEED TO KNOW

Just as artists gather tools such as paints and canvas, we can gather information about ourselves and God's activity in our lives. As you seek to identify your God-given purposes and begin to gather the data of your life, ask yourself:

- What childhood experiences tell me about who I am?
- What unusual things have I been curious about my entire life?
- What tendencies was I born with, apparently formed in my mother's womb (Psalm 139:13)?
- What in my life has broken my heart?
- How might God be helping all things work together for good in my life (Romans 8:28)?

One of the richest data sources is our past experience, especially events from childhood that shaped and formed us. Miriam Adeney, the cultural anthropologist first mentioned in chapter 4, illustrates Jesus' purpose of discipling the nations and urging all cultures to put their hope in Jesus' name (Matthew 12:21; 28:19-20). She fulfills her purpose through tasks such as teaching about other cultures, worshiping in multicultural situations, and directing a program that assists writers in other cultures in producing books. She credits part of her fascination with other cultures to the "data" of her childhood, especially living in Micronesia as a four-year-old when her father was a U.S. Navy doctor.

One of her friends was a navy steward, a Filipino man named Cesar. "Every day after the coffee break, we sat on the bench and talked about life," says Miriam. "He talked about how working for the Navy would help him make money so he could marry his girlfriend, Lilly. With all the ethnocentricity of an American, I protested that he shouldn't leave. 'But you have a good life with us here!' I thought working for Americans was the best thing that could happen to him. Why would he go anywhere else? But he helped me see that America is not the center of the world. That made an impression on me, even at the age of four."

Since that time, Miriam's fascination for culture has continued to grow. "I see the various cultures as a mosaic or kaleidoscope, a community of families," she says. "I see myself as part of that great body of families—delighting in that body, facilitating it, contributing to its growth and expansion."

Even negative experiences from childhood can be used as data. These experiences may not have been placed there by God, but he can salvage them in ways that enrich who we are. For JoeAnn Ballard, childhood experiences explain why she and her husband, Monroe, have felt so compelled to "encourage…and… listen…, defending the fatherless and the oppressed" (Psalm 10:17-18).

JoeAnn was the youngest of three children who drank their first milk from old Coca-Cola bottles and heard their parents squabbling instead of singing lullabies. When she was six weeks old, her parents separated. She was raised in a good but poor home as the last of DeLoach and Ora Mae Benjamin's forty-eight foster children. JoeAnn idolized her foster father, an industrious farmer disabled in World War II, who worked hard on their twelve-hundred-acre farm and pecan orchard in Lucedale, Mississippi. Her positive experience in a foster home helps explain why she and Monroe have served as foster parents to fifty-five children. In addition, at least 350 other children and teens who simply needed a place to stay have lived in their home for brief periods of time. Like JoeAnn's foster parents, she and her husband exchange no money with an agency. They just take kids in.

Another way JoeAnn comes alongside oppressed, fatherless people is through the eighteen Neighborhood Christian Centers (NCC) she founded in Memphis and northern Mississippi. The centers provide counseling, Bible clubs, emergency food, job assistance, clothing, furniture, and referrals to doctors and attorneys when needed. Two of the NCC's primary services are tutoring and reading programs, which is not surprising when you learn that JoeAnn's elementary school often ran out of textbooks; she learned to read while looking over other kids' shoulders. JoeAnn's deep gladness is to provide the encouragement and security for which the world hungers in the form of some things she had in childhood (a caring foster home) and other things she didn't have (the educational resources she needed).

As JoeAnn's life illustrates, even our brokenness needs to be valued and cherished because it gives us clues about how we can be a part of the "family business" of God. "There is a mysterious link between our brokenness and our ability to give to each other," wrote Henri Nouwen. "Just as bread needs to be broken in order to be given, so, too, do our lives."[2]

My friend Barbara Gage, whom I mentioned earlier is the administrator of a law firm, grew up in a home with abuse. As a young woman, she was raped and shot in the head. After recovering physically and then becoming a Christian, she worked through the fear and insecurity of these experiences, and now she's a quiet defender of people who are treated unjustly. The experiential "data" she's collected in life have molded her into a determined advocate of the oppressed. Her heart is broken by what breaks God's heart: "Defend the cause of the weak and fatherless; maintain the rights of the poor and oppressed" (Psalm 82:3).

PAYING ATTENTION

All of this rich data can elude us, which is why we need to be attentive to our lives. "Observe your life carefully, closely, and reverently," advises writer Jean Blomquist:

What gives you energy, joy, satisfaction? To what do you devote yourself fully and freely? Be attentive, especially in difficult situations. What might it mean to choose life here? Cultivate a willingness to wait—and not to wait. We need to balance the sacred skill of watchful waiting with holy risking. Discover and honor your "signals." Contemplate the words, wisdom, and challenges of others. What do your friends, co-workers, or family see in you that you cannot see? At the same time, listen to your own heart when you sense others may be leading you away from your God-given gladness. Finally, seek to quiet yourself in prayer that you may hear the "still, small voice" of God.[3]

Data collecting combines listening to yourself and others and laying all that before God. Here are some concrete ways to pay attention to the data of your life:

Journal about your experiences. When someone or something upsets you, write about it. Do you worry about kids who have nowhere to go after school? Does it bother you when a Christian writes a negative, harsh letter to the editor of your newspaper—do you wish the letters reflected Jesus' justice and mercy? What situations like these seem silly to others but important to you?

When journaling, don't worry about format, grammar, or even the regularity of writing in your journal; just write when you need to write. Apply to journaling the same principle Jesus applied to the Sabbath: "The Sabbath was made for man, not man for the Sabbath" (Mark 2:27).

Gather information. Identify your hot topics and start a folder for every topic that grips your heart, such as aging, alcoholism, apologetics. If you don't have material to put in the folders, make them anyway and you probably will find it. Then file anything that speaks to the deep part of yourself: newspaper articles, copied passages from books, notes about upsetting things people have said. To get yourself thinking about these topics, buy related books and tapes and attend related trade shows or conventions. If nothing else, start a folder labeled "Purpose," and throw in brochures of enticing activities or notes from unforgettable seminars. Then go through the file periodically, asking, *What is God saying to me? What may God be asking me to be involved in?*

Take a class. Before attending a conference or registering for a class, ask yourself what you hope to learn from it. If it's a writer's conference, do you need to build skills? Determine if writing is a life profession? Figure out how to fit it into your schedule? If it's a missions conference, do you need to make connections? Gather information? Be inspired? Talk with other attendees, invite one or two to lunch, and ask them your questions. Before the class ends, identify one or two steps you need to take.

If you have no idea what your purpose is but a certain task appeals to you, pursue it. Explore it and see why it excites you. Of course certain tasks (become a therapist; work as an ecologist) may require you to enroll in college or get an advanced degree. But take heart; going back to school may not be as difficult as you think. At age fifty, *USA Today* columnist Barbara Reynolds found graduate school easier than college. "This time, I had money, credit cards, a car. I didn't have to worry about boyfriends." She had to work, of course, as a columnist facing a deadline every other day. "But that was nothing compared to struggling for identity as a teenager."[4]

And when you show up for classes, you'll find many women there over the age of twenty-two. As of 1991, more than twelve hundred women aged fifty to sixty-four were studying in the United States for their first professional degrees, seriously applying themselves to law, dentistry, pharmacy, social psychology, or divinity schools.[5] Fordham University in New York has even started a "College at 60 Program."

Help someone who's doing what you want to do. Take a position as a volunteer or an intern at an organization related to your interest. By active participation, you'll discover if your heart is truly broken by this cause or if it simply interests you. You'll discover what temperament and skills are needed for various purpose-related tasks. As you help, ask the person you're assisting, "How did you start out doing this? What skills or qualities do you think are essential? If you had to go back to school, how did you manage?" (For a list of directories of internships and other tools for experimenting, see Appendix B of Richard Nelson Bolles's book, *What Color Is Your Parachute?*)

Take stock of your skills—even unrelated ones. Evaluate "what is." Look at the you God created. What aptitudes do you have? What strengths and skills have you acquired? Take personality and temperament tests. What education do you have, including miscellaneous, seemingly irrelevant classes?

KEEPING AN OPEN HEART

Data collection works best when we see ourselves as perpetual learners, researchers, and experimenters. The challenge is to remain open to God's leading and risk talking to someone about ideas that scare us or seem unconventional. For example, you might say to yourself: *Okay, I'm a teacher, but part of me is drawn to carpentry and woodworking. What's that about? What's going on inside me, God? What does this tell me about my purpose in life?*

Fortunately for us, Sheila Lichacz (pronounced Shay-la Leh-shays) kept this sort of open heart. During her freshman year in college she heard a staff member say to female students, "Make the most of yourself because you'll never happen again." Twenty years later, Sheila Lichacz sat on the platform at that same university to be honored as Outstanding Alumni of the Year. The accomplishment that prompted this honor had nothing to do with home economics (her college major), her subsequent master's degree, or the job she acquired as a school guidance counselor.

Sheila's "outstanding" work is that of an artist. Her work flows from her purpose in life—communicating the love of God in a way others can see and touch ("Show the wonder of [God's] great love," Psalm 17:7, NIV; see also Romans 5:5, KJV). Her paintings and montages* have been exhibited in highly esteemed places such as the Museum of Modern Art of Latin America in Washington, D.C., and Dudley House at Harvard University. Her life also shows us why we, in a culture that craves bottom-line realities, need to

---

*A montage is a picture formed by applying separate images in parts or layers; Sheila's layers often include pieces of pottery and shells.

keep the eraser ready to rub out our big plans and replace them with the purpose in which "your deep gladness and the world's deep hunger meet."[6]

Artists whose work focuses on religious themes don't often find much appreciation in the art world, but Sheila has. Her biblical scenes with names such as *Miracle at Cana, And I Will Raise Him Up* and *30 Pieces of Silver* don't portray human figures but everyday objects that represent people. These objects seem to come to life and move, hinting at divine undercurrents of joy, purpose, and connectedness while communicating the feel and tone of dramatic biblical events.

The everyday object that appears most often in her work is the simple clay pot. Why? As a child, Sheila played in the Rio Santa Maria in Panama and pulled shards of ancient pottery out of the river. (Her childhood home, Monagrillo, Panama, was the birthplace of ceramics in 3000 B.C.) Because she collected these shards as a child, she has studied archaeology and anthropology for years, putting segments of those shards on the canvas of her montages and using the image of the clay vessel as a central theme in her paintings.

Believers and nonbelievers alike are astounded at the obvious spirituality in Sheila's work. I believe it comes across so clearly without being preachy because she expresses it through the ways in which God has worked so uniquely in her life. These shards are part of the data pointing to Sheila's purposes. Her deep gladness in them meets the world's deep hunger to know that broken things can be shaped and loved by God into something beautiful—and viewers of her work sense that.

When we remain open to how childhood aspirations may have shaped our paths, we may discover coincidences we hadn't noticed before. For example, as I read *A Time for Remembering*, a biography of Ruth Bell Graham who grew up in China with missionary parents, I was struck by her childhood dream of being a single missionary to the nomads of Tibet, living high on a mountain far from civilization at the "roof of the globe." You might think that as the wife of Billy Graham, she never came close to that. But I think she did. She managed to build a home of century-old logs on an obscure ridge in the mountains of North Carolina. From that haven for her well-known family, she has spun out in ministry. By teaching the college Sunday school class at nearby Anderson-Montreat College, she came in touch with all types of young adults, both bikers and scholars. While politicians and celebrities visited the Graham home, it was "the lonely, the misfits that Ruth welcomed with special warmth and virtually adopted."

This woman, who as a child encountered abandoned, dying babies as she walked to school in China, has not found it unusual to befriend a prostitute or a murderer and continue to "involve herself with people who were beyond her help" in others' eyes. Well-known to the local police, "she was often the first to visit the prisoner or appear at the scene of the crime; like her father (a missionary doctor), her impulse was not to judge, but to heal."[7] Despite all that came to her, Ruth Bell Graham did not lay aside the longings of her childhood heart.

Perhaps you're examining your life but no red thread of purpose appears. You've collected the data and it looks like a junk heap. Don't be discouraged. Perspective takes time. When and how, I wonder, did Moses realize his purpose in life? Perhaps by the beginning of the journey to the Promised Land, he may have realized that his purpose was to deliver Israel: physically from Egypt to the Promised Land; spiritually from a passive slavery mind-set to an active willingness to bless all nations. But at the burning bush, Moses seemed to be clueless. He even told God he didn't want to deliver Israel. But the fact was, Moses' purpose was already so infused in him that years earlier he'd tried to deliver Israel—on a small scale and in a blunderbuss way—by secretly killing an Egyptian in order to free one Hebrew from a beating (Exodus 2:11-12; 3:11). Moses had then left town, grown up, and inevitably talked heart-to-heart with God while herding sheep (good preparation for herding a nation). By the time he arrived back in Egypt, God had enlarged his role in delivering the Hebrews. Now, Moses would openly free all Hebrews.

Like Moses, you may have blundered through your purposes until they're unrecognizable. But I encourage you to collect the data anyway, realizing that your failures may be your best source of material.

QUESTIONS TO PONDER OR DISCUSS

1. Reflect on your favorite movies and books, especially from childhood. What stories and fictional or real-life characters inspire you?

2. What are some steps you're willing to take to investigate your interests? to collect data?

3. Have you had painful experiences that can prod you in a new direction?

EXPERIMENT IN LISTENING PRAYER

Ask God, *What ideas and themes have repeated themselves throughout my life?*

BIBLE PASSAGE TO CONTEMPLATE

> Praise be to the God and Father of our Lord Jesus Christ, the Father of compassion and the God of all comfort, who comforts us in all our troubles, so that we can comfort those in any trouble with the comfort we ourselves have received from God. For just as the sufferings of Christ flow over into our lives, so also through Christ our comfort overflows. If we are distressed, it is for your comfort and salvation; if we are comforted, it is for your comfort, which produces in you patient endurance of the same sufferings we suffer. And our hope for you is firm, because we know that just as you share in our sufferings, so also you share in our comfort. (2 Corinthians 1:3-7)

SEVEN

THE STAGES
OF DISCOVERY

Christina Riccardi and her husband were separated for several years. During that period when she lived as a single mother of three boys, Christina often used up her food stamps and wondered where the next gallon of milk would come from. "I felt so isolated and alone, and I saw how much I needed other women," says Christina. "Eventually my husband and I got back together. By that time I'd learned a lot about how to care about people, especially about listening instead of giving advice."

This woman loved God and wanted to serve him—but how? When Christina heard about a local crisis pregnancy center, she thought about the abortions of her past and grieved for the loneliness of the women there. "I could identify with them and their need for support and encouragement. My heart longed to be involved, but with my low self-worth I knew they wouldn't want me as a volunteer." Besides, she was a mother of small children. What could she do?

Christina's restless feelings are typical of the second phase in the discovery process.

PHASE 2: INCUBATION—LETTING THE DATA COALESCE

The data we gather develops and gestates, growing slowly under the light of God's love, but during the incubation period it may look and feel as if nothing is happening. Therapists Mary Braheny and Diane Halperin say that people want to hurry up and get over the incubation phase because it feels like depression instead of progression. Says Mary, "[The process of identifying your purpose in life is] like making a pot of soup. All the flavors blend. The chicken and seasonings are in there, but it has to boil long enough for all the flavors to come together to taste like chicken soup. Even at a low simmer, the liquid brews and gets tumultuous. In the same way, people get nervous about this stage. They feel it's a journey downward from which they will never come back."

Lifting the lid to see if the soup is ready doesn't help. The more we try to figure it out, the more frustrated we may become. Perfectionists, especially, are brutal with themselves during this period. They want to figure out their purposes in life now, but this incubation phase is a time to play around with ideas and mull over the data we've collected.

In this percolation process, ideas often rise to the top and then become a part of the mix in the heart. Questions such as, *What have I come to the kingdom for? What breaks my heart that breaks the heart of God?* need to be played with for unintentional meditation to occur. The goal is to stay focused on discovering our purpose without troubling ourselves over it. When our purpose finally occurs to us, we think, *I knew that!*

It's disconcerting that it should take so long to discover a purpose already burning in our hearts. But until we deliberately begin the process, we're aware of our purposes only on certain levels. God's purposes may be clear, but the *how* or *when* is incubating. The apostle Paul's purpose of reaching the Gentiles was explicit from the beginning, but he still spent three years in Arabia for reasons not explained to us (Acts 9:15; Galatians 1:17-18).

ACTIVE WAITING

Incubation is a period of preparation and active waiting, described well in Hebrews 12:1: "Let us *run* with *patience* the race that is set before us" (KJV, emphasis added). Have you ever seen someone run patiently? This isn't what we see at short track-meet events, but rather at cross-country meets or marathons in which runners pace themselves for long distances. Active waiting is like this. We ponder our purposes in life, paying attention to whatever's in front of us and listening for more input.

While we wait, we can take four specific actions:

Ask, What if? In your conversations with God, let the question, *What if…?* play itself out in your head. Before Bill Bowerman invented the airsole unit of Nike shoes, he asked himself, "What happens if I pour rubber into a waffle iron?" Albert Einstein wondered, "What would a light wave look like if someone was keeping pace with it?"[1] Ask yourself, *What if God called me to…? What if someone came to me and offered to…? What if I quit my job and…?*

Participate in activities in which time flies. During what activity does time seem to stand still or is totally forgotten? These timeless activities are important in discovering our purposes because they create open spaces in which we are likely to hear God speak through the words of a friend or a new thought. Three settings in which this feeling of timelessness often occurs are:

- close relationships (lunch with a good friend)
- immersion in creative activities (including artistic activities, such as painting or composing, as well as anything that forces you to be innovative—fixing a tape recorder with a homemade part, thinking up a new format for a Sunday school class, or preparing something original for breakfast)
- worship (wishing your time of personal prayer or corporate worship would never end)[2]

During these timeless moments, ideas are likely to occur to you. Old longings of the heart may surface. Thoughts and feelings often coalesce so that your purposes become clear.

Notice which doors close. When I beat on a door and it doesn't open, maybe it's not supposed to. God's guidance is sometimes made more clear in what doesn't happen than what does. Once I've accepted that a door has closed and I am no longer preoccupied with it, I may notice another nearby door that's standing wide open. Until a door opens, I can move forward with what I know. It's interesting that Paul didn't receive his vision to go to Macedonia until he and his companions were already on their journey and doors had closed to Asia and Bithynia (Acts 16:6-10). In the midst of their going, God gave them direction. In the same way, as we explore the *what* of our purpose, God will probably reveal the *how, when,* and *where.*

Author Parker Palmer talks about closed doors, calling them a "way closing" behind us. Perseverance is important, he says, but "when I constantly refuse to take no for an answer, I miss the vital clues that God gives me when [the] 'way closes.'"[3]

Palmer tells of being fired from a summer research job for poor performance. He not only lost his summer income, but his entire graduate program was in jeopardy. He admitted he hadn't worked hard enough and had even thought that the work project was a joke. Did that prompt a lack of concentration? "I did not work hard enough to deserve that job, so I lost it," Palmer says. "But that truth does not go deep enough—not if I am to discover the meaning of a 'way closing' behind me. I can see now that I was fired because that job had little or nothing to do with who I really am, with my true nature and gifts, with what I care and do not care about, and my resort to humor reflected that simple fact....At that time, I did not understand my soul....It would be nice if our limits did not reveal themselves in such embarrassing, even shameful, ways as getting fired from a job. But if you are like me, you don't easily acknowledge your limits. Shame and embarrassment may be the only ways to get your attention."[4]

Let your healing take shape. To seek purpose may mean facing something that has been too overwhelming, too heartbreaking, or too distasteful. This confrontation cannot be forced, but can be found by walking humbly with God. Christina Riccardi had been reconciled with her husband for a few years when she first heard about the local crisis pregnancy center (CPC), but she knew she wasn't ready to get involved. "A few years later when the CPC director appealed for volunteers at church, I went to the CPC, sat at the director's desk, and said, 'I'll do whatever you need me to do. I've had abortions, but God has healed my heart and I truly know the deep forgiveness of God. I'm passing that on to my children and I want to pass it on to others. I think I am ready to minister at your center.'"

The director was in need of board members—would Christina consider it? "That night on the way home I broke out into such a cry I could hardly breathe. God was using me for his purpose—using my past sin to his glory in helping others! The board needed a secretary, and I've been their secretary for ten years now. It's a perfect job for me. I don't get burned out because of the joy and excitement I get doing the thing that's in my heart that's so important. It helps complete my healing."

This volunteer slot frequently has placed Christina within elbow-rubbing proximity of women who need her purpose of announcing how God has forgiven her and redeemed her life. "Announce this with shouts of joy and proclaim it. Send it out to the ends of the earth; say, 'The LORD has redeemed his servant Jacob'" (Isaiah 48:20). Christina fulfills her purpose of bringing hurting women to Christ in other ways as well, such as leading Bible studies, one of which is for the women in her neighborhood, and meeting with other moms for prayer on Saturday mornings at 7:00 A.M. "I want to be a listening friend to other women, especially the ones who are hurting as I was."

PHASE 3: ILLUMINATION—THE "AHA" MOMENT

This may occur as an astonishing "That's it!" moment or as a series of small breakthroughs. Either way, we figure out, *This is how I'm to be a part of the "family business"!* We feel an inward trust that we know what's going on. We abandon the old path we were on and strike out anew. Author Virginia Woolf called such little epiphanies "moments of being," when a "shock pulls the gauzy curtain off everyday existence and throws a sudden floodlight on what our lives are really about."[5]

For Christina Riccardi, working with the CPC was a breakthrough, or an "aha" moment, in which her purpose became clear as she risked to perform a new kind of task. As she became more confident, she began bonding with the hurting women at the center. She saw this as a response to her own years of isolation, and she came to realize that in these relationships she was partnering with God in his redemptive purposes.

"Aha" moments are often ignited by something we've known or suspected for a long time, but it comes to light because of a calamity or comment. Henrietta Mears, with her strong background in education, was set aflame by a comment from a Phi Beta Kappa student who said, "What's wrong, Miss Mears? I've gone to Sunday school all of my life, but if I had to take an examination on the Bible today, I'd flunk." Triggered by such comments, "Miss Mears and her educators worked out a prospectus [for closely graded curriculum, meaning different methods for different grades], determining the accomplishments expected at each age level."[6] This curriculum was revolutionary in its time and became the foundation for a new Christian publishing house, Gospel Light Publications. No doubt, comments such as this one also fueled Henrietta Mears's desire to study hard to teach her college classes, and as a result there was standing room only outside her classroom door.

Painful experiences may force us into a breakthrough. Artist Sheila Lichacz, whom you met in the last chapter, quit her job as a guidance counselor after a student spit on her. Her husband, then a U.S. Air Force officer, was stationed in the Panama Canal Zone, and Sheila, a native Panamanian and U.S. citizen, was teaching school there. At that time, Americans didn't want Panamanians in the Canal Zone. She told me, "After the student spit in my face, I washed my face, but the spit stays with you. I decided I could never teach again."

Not sure what to do, Sheila went to Canal Zone College. "I enrolled in Art 101—me, with a master's degree in guidance counseling! The instructor hated my paintings of trees and landscapes. She told me I would fail the course. I wanted to drop the class, but it was past the time to do so." Then Sheila painted a clay pot, like the vessels from her childhood. "The teacher liked it so much she asked me who helped me with it! I kept working."

Within four years of this "aha" moment in which she realized she could gather material from her childhood to create art, the president of Panama honored Sheila as "The Pride of Panama and the Americas" because of her paintings.

When one opportunity dies, it frees a space for God to move his purposes into our field of vision. And when a breakthrough comes in a series of experiences, it may take awhile to see the entire picture. You may feel forlorn that your backyard Bible study with kids is over or that you no longer hear well enough to sing in the choir, but try to think of these disappointments as places in which God can speak to you. He seems to give us only enough light for the next few steps. Much like the master in the parable of the talents, he gives us only one or two or five steps to take at a time (Matthew 25:14-30). Our job is to walk obediently in the light God gives us today.

TEST YOUR IDEA ON A SMALL SCALE

While discovering our purposes can take a long time, we can't postpone action indefinitely. As soon as we can find the courage, it's time to dabble in the purposes we have discovered in our "aha" moments. The first step is to find low-risk ways to try it out and solicit realistic feedback. Is God pulling you toward a purpose that involves making crafts? Participate in a holiday boutique. Is God pulling you toward a purpose that involves foster kids? Be a relief foster parent for a weekend and try it. Do you want to go overseas as a missionary? Take a short missions trip.

It's not a bad idea to start small. For example, Elizabeth Fry began by praying. As a Quaker wife in the early 1800s, her days were consumed with household duties, including the tasks involved in rearing eleven children. But Elizabeth felt guilty for not being "a useful instrument," and she began to look outward for service. Her search ended at the nearby Newgate Prison—"a notorious hell-hole with a reputation for dehumanizing its inmates."[7]

"Fry's ministry at Newgate began with a humble request to the prison governor: 'Sir, if thee kindly allows me to pray with the women [prisoners], I will go inside.' Once inside, however, she quickly realized that the ministry would involve much more than prayer. With the help of friends, she brought food and clothing to the starving and naked inmates, but she concentrated her efforts on employment and education in an attempt to eradicate the 'vicious idleness' that had become a way of life behind the prison walls. So effective were her efforts that Newgate became a showcase for prison reform, and she was recognized worldwide for her self-giving Christian ministry."[8]

I can imagine Elizabeth Fry moving one step at a time with the light she had. Praying led to doing, which led to a showcase ministry. We think that our purposes in life need a grand beginning. It might be enough to pray with other women.

PHASE 4: VERIFICATION—LOOKING AT THE RESULTS

After you've launched a project or even mentioned to your friend what you think your purpose might be, what response do you get? When others say, "What you said moved me," or "This conference you led is the best one I've attended," it *might* be an indication that you're discovering your purpose. Don't worry if the confirmation doesn't come from the most prestigious places, but look for it from those whose opinion you value. "When we're authentic, others usually perceive us as such and will often go to great lengths to help us succeed."[9]

Success, however, is never the barometer for purpose in life. Vincent van Gogh's art was just as moving in his lifetime, when he was rejected, as it is now. The best verification is to take the comments of others back to our ongoing conversation with God and ask him to help us be discerning in our evaluation of results.

When we are exercising our God-given purpose, we should hear an inner yes that has nothing to do with self-glorification. Be on guard for this thought: *When I do this, people look up to me.* Set it aside and pray in whatever position necessary to relinquish these issues—bent over, on your knees, lying face down in the carpet. Our goal is never self-realization or destiny, but fellowship with God.

In each phase, the excitement comes not from having achieved levels of awareness or even from finding our purpose. (In fact, phase four can be uncomfortably stretching!) The joy always comes from interacting with God, who is eager to bring us on board his redemptive purposes.

QUESTIONS TO PONDER OR DISCUSS

1. What activities make time fly for you?
2. What ideas do you need to test on a small scale?
3. When have you received verification that something you've done may be connected to God's purposes for your life?

EXPERIMENT IN LISTENING PRAYER

Consider a time when people have given you positive feedback about something you've done and ask God these questions:

- *Do I have a sense of rightness about it all?*
- *Do I have a sense of your leading me?*
- *Do I have a sense of selflessness—this isn't about me, is this about you?*

BIBLE PASSAGE TO CONTEMPLATE

Notice how the apostle Paul never shrank from making purpose statements; he stated his specific purposes to people:

> My *purpose* is that they may be encouraged in heart and united in love, so that they may have the full riches of complete understanding, in order that they may know the mystery of God, namely, Christ. (Colossians 2:2, emphasis added)

> I am sending him to you for the express *purpose* that you may know about our circumstances and that he may encourage your hearts. (Colossians 4:8, emphasis added)

EIGHT

STATING YOUR MISSION

Some people find that each of their purposes in life falls neatly under a phrase. Together, these phrases can be crystallized into a short statement that encompasses and describes their purposes in life. This is often called a mission statement or a purpose statement. For example, in chapter 3, I noted Christine Sine's purpose statement: "I want to be a voice to the voiceless, to assist people at the bottom end of the ladder and be a spokesperson for those who are in some way excluded." In her book *Tales of a Seasick Doctor,* she quoted the biblical rationale for this purpose: "'Speak up for those who cannot speak for themselves, for the rights of all who are destitute. Speak up and judge fairly; defend the rights of the poor and needy,' proclaims Proverbs 31:8-9, piercing my heart with the cry from those who are helpless."[1]

In her book *The Path: Creating Your Mission Statement for Work and for Life,* Laurie Beth Jones says, "A mission statement should be no more than a single sentence long. It should be easily understood by a twelve-year-old. It should be able to be recited by memory at gunpoint."[2] Although you've read the long version of my purpose statements, the short versions roll off my tongue easily: authentic spirituality, social justice, substance over glitz, pastors' families. I see these phrases so frequently on my office whiteboard (and I've made so many difficult decisions based on them) that I can rattle them off easily.

I prefer general mission statements that don't name specific tasks. Broad wording assumes the purposes will permeate every role in life—employee, neighbor, daughter, spouse, parent, volunteer, church member, or board member of professional or neighborhood organization. No matter what we do, the things we are passionate about flow from our mouths and become apparent to those with whom we interact. Your purposes are more than what you *do;* they encompass who God has called you to *be.* Here are some examples of thematic mission statements:

- Providing safety for the brokenhearted.
- Speaking truth in places where God's name is not known.
- Promoting harmony among those who disagree.

Although these purposes are broad, they name specifically the target of their mission: the brokenhearted, places where God's name is not known, and those who disagree.

It would be easy to get hooked on fancy wording for a statement, but I prefer to concern myself more with listening to God and less with format. However, mission statements vary widely, and I wouldn't presume to dictate one way to write it. Just to get started, I'd suggest putting your purposes on paper in any way that works. Then let your mission statement grow and change as it becomes more clear.

Some people recommend including long pages of thoughts[3]; others suggest linking your mission statement with a specific task. This is often helpful with early versions of a mission statement. Women in the Bible study I led told me I "made the Bible come alive," so I put that phrase at the top of my résumé and added it to letters pitching myself as a curriculum writer. Here are some other examples of task-related mission statements:

- Create pure foods to help people's bodies not get in the way of their spiritual growth.
- Make fine harps so people hear the voice of God in the wind.
- Make people laugh so the travail of earthly life doesn't seem so hard.
- Help people know the truth about what is happening out in the world to promote honesty in the world.
- Create beautiful gardens so people may behold the beauty of God and be reminded of the beauty of holiness.[4]

My own mission statement grew and changed as I came to a place of brokenness in my life, as I began to see the damage I'd caused my husband and children with my continual attempts to do everything right and force *them* to do everything right. Sitting in support groups and hearing others talk, I worked at confessing sin, surrendering character flaws, and becoming accountable to fellow strugglers. My heart was ripped open in these settings, and I knew I'd come "home," not only to God in the "prodigal son" sense, but also to his purposes in some way. In time, I saw that a better statement of my purpose would be: "Presenting God in an authentic way, especially to hurting people" (of whom I am one). This involved many tasks, such as setting up chairs for support groups, listening to people's stories, interacting one-on-one with women as I speak at retreats, writing books that speak of faith in an authentic way (some of which are directed to hurting groups of people), and praying for my teenagers' friends as they explore my kitchen and occupy the back seat of my car. My mission statement went on to include the items listed in chapter 3.

While you're working out your own statement, you may want to use scriptural phrases and ideas. My purpose of promoting authentic spirituality comes from Philippians 3:10: "To know Christ and the power of his resurrection." This grew out of my being upset that people seem hooked on formulas for being spiritual rather than on the person of Christ. I saw how this leads to self-satisfaction rather than a dying to self, "the fellowship of sharing in his sufferings, becoming like him in his death" (Philippians 3:10). Perhaps you'd like to review the purposes of God listed in chapter 5 and look for wording that matches biblical big-picture ideas.

THE POSITIVE SPIN

It's easy to think of purpose in terms of what's wrong with the world. We feel annoyed or angry or grieved as we read the newspaper, so we think:
- If I could change the world...
- If I could change the church...
- If I could change the way certain people are treated...
- If I could change the way people treat themselves...
- If I could change the way God is perceived in this world...

If what breaks your heart leads you to feel emotionally upset or angry, ask God to focus your anger in a positive way, shaping it into the "passion" portion of compassion. In my own grief over racial prejudice, I was so upset that my purpose had little forward movement. I needed to be *for* something true, noble, right, pure, lovely, or admirable (Philippians 4:8), but I had a hard time phrasing my purpose in a positive statement. I considered the popular idea that people should be "color-blind," in other words, not taking notice of individual race. But I believe that denies the truth that everyone has an ethnicity of which we each have a right to be proud. As my networking with like-thinkers increased, I came to embrace my purpose in biblical terms—racial reconciliation.

So often we find ourselves asking, *What is wrong?* The more important question is, *How does God wish to make this right?* Finding the positive spin on a negative situation is the redemptive edge of purpose in life. One example of this is Frances Willard, one of the foremost leaders of the temperance movement (1839–98). While temperance would appear to be a negative issue—*Stop drinking*—Frances did not view it that way. The Women's Christian Temperance Union had a much bigger vision, including evangelistic outreach to men. This international organization, comprised of thousands of women, operated on local levels and "sponsored Bible reading and gospel work in prisons and in police stations among railroad employees, soldiers, sailors and lumberman."[5] Frances Willard did not focus on what people shouldn't be doing, but on what they could do to know Christ and behave with integrity and empathy.

This energetic dynamo was active in the women's suffrage movement. But Frances Willard wasn't just a busybody or a do-gooder; all of her activity grew out of a relationship with God. So vivid was this relationship that she also conducted afternoon Bible lectures, often speaking on "the unsearchable riches of Christ" (Ephesians 3:8, KJV). She was even invited by evangelist Dwight L. Moody to preach at a Sunday afternoon meeting, and it was in a letter to Mrs. D. L. Moody that Frances wrote what appears to have been her mission statement: "All my life I have been devoted to the advancement of women in education and opportunity."[6] So was Jesus, based on the way he dared to talk to women about spiritual matters in a time when that sort of thing simply wasn't done.

TELL OTHERS YOUR LIFE PURPOSES

Several years after I'd begun focusing on my purposes, I made a friend at a relief and development organization, and we talked a lot about ministry to the poor and oppressed overseas. Suddenly, it dawned on me that my editors considered me a journalist competent to write about many topics, but they didn't know what meant the most to me. Wasn't it time I told them about my purposes in life? If I did so, perhaps my name would come up at editorial meetings when they discussed an idea related to authentic spirituality or social justice.

So I taped a copy of my purpose statements next to the telephone. In every conversation with an editor, I tagged that statement onto the end. I got used to saying it, and I found it easier to turn down speaking engagements that weren't in line with my purposes. I'd say, "No, but here's what I'm about," and then I'd give my purpose statement. I changed my résumé and my speaker's flyer to focus specifically on my purposes. Somehow I hadn't thought of all those things until I began stating my purposes aloud to my friend.

Even when we're hammering away at our purposes, we may tend to forget them in the midst of life's busyness. After I'd printed mine on a whiteboard in my workspace, I hemmed and hawed when asked to write an article on five areas of the United States that have Third-World living standards (high rate of hunger, infant deaths, and so on). I hedged because it would take an enormous amount of research. A day later, it hit me. For more than a year, I'd asked God for assignments to write about social justice—how could I turn this down? I took the assignment and wrote the article. That project resulted in more calls for such articles, and I've used the research from that piece many times. I looked my "verification" in the face and almost denied it.

UH OH...I STILL DON'T GET IT

Before we close this section on discovering our purposes, I want to address anyone who may be thinking, *I still have no idea what my purpose is!* I urge you to keep investigating your skills and spiritual gifts and asking God how they fit with what's in your heart. Learn how to keep your own living space organized, how you fit best in an organization or event, how to get your point across to people. These experiences will help you understand the aptitudes God has given you. In my twenties, I decided to say yes to everything I was asked to do—for a while. I directed conferences, led a choir (without any training!), and even became president of a group for pastors' wives, of which I was the youngest member. I made mistakes and learned a lot about myself, so when my purposes began surfacing, I had some idea of how to proceed. I'd organized enough seminars and meetings, for example, to know my joy lay elsewhere. This became part of the valuable "data collection" process.

Another place to explore is the special "moments" in Scripture that draw you. Who is your favorite Bible character? What passage has a phrase in it you can cite verbatim without having tried to memorize it? Whatever attracts you probably describes something about God that fascinates you. If you can't think of anything, try reading a gospel in one sitting (Mark is the shortest) and then recall your favorite scenes. What divine purposes were embodied in those scenes?

Sometimes you know what breaks your heart, but it never appears in Scripture. Look for an event in Scripture with similar issues. Let's say hospice work draws you. What is God's heart for the dying? Christ spent a lot of time with lepers—people who were doomed to a slow death. You may not be able to heal the dying or raise the dead to life as Christ did, but in the spirit of Christ, you can care for people facing death and love them, even introducing them to the kingdom of God.

Even when we know our purposes, we may have to wait for doors to open. After the shepherd David was anointed king, you would expect that he would have entered the royal court in an executive capacity, right? No, he gained entrance as a harp player (1 Samuel 16:14-23). He probably did not become king for more than ten years.[7] In the same way, we look at our burden for the Haitian people or love of theater or ability to climb a rock, and we develop it to God's glory. This gift or burden may open a door. A church may be planning a mission trip to Haiti or a reenactment of a gospel scene or a high-adventure trip and ask you to help. In the midst of the activity, "your ears will hear a voice behind you, saying, 'This is the way; walk in it'" (Isaiah 30:21).

Listen prayerfully for that voice.

QUESTIONS TO PONDER OR DISCUSS

1. Eric Liddell loved missionary work, and he loved running. Somehow, those two things didn't conflict for Liddell, even though his sister thought so. He said, "I believe that God made me for a purpose. For [missionary work]. But He also made me fast, and when I run, I feel His pleasure. To give it up would be to hold Him in contempt. To win is to honor Him."[8] What gives you "God's pleasure"?
2. Write down a few phrases you might want to consider in a mission statement.

EXPERIMENT IN LISTENING PRAYER

Ask God, *How can I partner with you in promoting mercy, justice, and a humble walk with you?*

BIBLE PASSAGE TO CONTEMPLATE

> For he himself is our peace, who has made the two one and has destroyed the barrier, the dividing wall of *hostility*, by abolishing in his flesh the law with its commandments and regulations. His purpose was to create in himself one new man out of the two, thus making peace, and in this one body to reconcile both of them to God through the cross, by which he put to death their *hostility*. (Ephesians 2:14-16, emphasis added)

MOVING DOWN THE ROAD

NINE

A HEART FOR GOD

enrietta Mears is known for all she did in God's kingdom (developing a huge Sunday school, discipling leaders, founding Forest Home Conference Center). Yet amid all her doing she positioned herself frequently at the feet of God—studying, listening, enjoying him. Even in her busy schedule, Ms. Mears's times of solitude with God were regular but intense: "She opened her Bible in the sacred silence of personal fellowship with God with much the same attention as a starving man approaches a banquet."[1] At death she was depicted as having "slipped through the veil between the present and the hereafter, which she had described over the years as being so very, very thin. Someone remarked, 'It was nothing new to meet her Lord alone, for she had often done so. This time she just went with him.'"[2]

Henrietta Mears was both "Martha the doer" and "Mary the lover." A slogan she used often was "to know Christ and make him known," and she was good at *being* (having a personal relationship with God) and *doing* (making him known).

The previous section was about discovering our purposes, and as we're working on that, it's important to pay attention to the foundational work necessary to move forward with those purposes. This third section focuses on what we need to know, be, and do if our purposes are to flourish into a God-driven, passionate, but selfless movement in our lives. If we don't become like the fertile soil in which a root of purpose can easily grow, we decay into shallow, rocky terrain that stifles purpose or into thorny soil that kills it

(Matthew 13:3-9). Many purpose-filled people have turned away from their mission because they lost their connection with God or their passion. They never developed the partners or skills they needed, or they tripped up on issues of self and inner neediness.

So what does it take to develop deep, rock-free, weed-free soil in which diligent "doing" grows from cultivated "being"?

A core intimacy with God nurtures a foundation in which purpose can flourish. Doing, doing, doing does not work—even nonreligious writers recognize this, and so they tie spirituality to purpose in life, using words such as *higher self, a silent partner within, the sleeping giant within me*.[3] For the Christian, the source of spirituality is God, who never forsakes us. "God is nearer to us than our own Soul," wrote Julian of Norwich.[4]

Our passion to work for God must never get ahead of seeking God for himself. The scriptural principle is: "For to me, to live is Christ" (Philippians 1:21). It's not, "For to me, to live is to *serve*," or "For to me, to live is to *do good*." The main focus of our lives is not achieving or being a peak performer or even working hard for God; it's knowing Christ.

A CONSTANT TURNING OVER OF SELF TO GOD

A life rooted in God combines intimacy and mission, knowledge and action, pulling in and pushing forward, soaking in and giving out, absorbing God and shedding self. It means pressing on while we're letting go, allowing our drivenness to give way to the path of God. It means listening carefully for his leading.

Artist Sheila Lichacz does this as she paints. "I pray before I start painting and I offer the work to God. I print a Latin abbreviation for the phrase 'To the greater glory of God' on the canvas, and I can almost feel God's hand guiding me. I grab the pastels with my fingers and it's as if I sculpt on canvas. My pastels talk to you, while my oils shout at you. My painting is a continuous prayer. I think of God and I sing to God. I talk to God like I'm talking to you. I enjoy it so much.

"I want my paintings to touch people and to bring them close to God. I share from my soul. If I planned out my paintings and charged certain amounts for them, they would be a flop. I paint for the honor and glory of God."

Working with a heart of prayer, as Sheila describes, requires a constant surrendering of self to God. As we learned in chapter 2, doing and being are intertwined. Let's say I'm serving on a committee related to my purpose. As a meeting is about to occur, I have bad vibrations about one woman's attitude. I can't tell whether she intimidates me or I intimidate her, but I wish she wouldn't show up. We're probably both willful people who think we're right. No wonder our short conversation in the hallway a few minutes ago was punctuated with little flashes of my-way-of-doing-it-is-better-isms. Now before I meet with her, I can run to an empty room and turn myself over to God once more: *Show me my attitudes that are self-promoting. Show me this woman's heart. Help me to listen to her and be interested in her—not just what she can do for me or my business or my church or my kids.* My purpose bears fruit only as long as my actions flow out of my relationship with God: "We cannot do a single good act except God first gives us the desire for it and then empowers us to do it."[5]

Please don't make the mistake of thinking this book is about having a destiny or pursuing a plan or working for a cause or finding a career. This book is about having a relationship with God in which we listen. We hear what God says to us, and we say yes. And then we keep saying yes every day to this Being who loves us desperately and has called us to sprint alongside him for the rest of our lives—and beyond.

A contemplative life with God prevents *self-congratulation.* As we follow our purposes, others will notice, admire us, and perhaps want to crown us as celebrities. Jesus showed us that in those moments it's good to get away and be with God (John 6:15).

Contemplation also prevents *burnout,* says Jim Wallis of the Sojourners community, which works with gangs in Washington, D.C.:

> Action without reflection can easily become barren and even
> bitter. Without the space for self-examination and the capacity

for rejuvenation, the danger of exhaustion and despair is too great. Contemplation confronts us with the questions of our identity and power. Who are we? To whom do we belong? Is there a power that is greater than ours? How can we know it? Our drivenness must give way to peacefulness and our anxiety to joy. So concerned with effectiveness, we learn instead to be content with faithfulness. Strategy grows into trust, success into obedience, planning into prayer.[6]

When a living, breathing relationship with God gets us out of bed in the morning, we are less likely to live for applause or brood over rejection. After the disciples successfully cast out demons (I would have sent out a press release on that for sure!), Jesus asked them not to focus on the dazzling power they had displayed or even on the people they had healed. Instead, he urged them to "rejoice that your names are written in heaven" (Luke 10:17-20). Their names recorded in heavenly script signified a solid connection with the divine being who treasured them. This connection with God is always the focus in purpose-full living.

HOW SOLITUDE HELPS

Whenever we're involved in purpose, it's easy to be shaped by other people's opinions about what we should and shouldn't do. Time alone with God helps us set aside the influences that tell us what we should do and what we should want—women's magazines, our friend's lifestyle, our sister's suggestions. As we continue on our journey to pursue the purpose we believe God has placed in our hearts, we can set aside the plans others have for us.

When my husband began pastoring a different church, he explained that I am sometimes absent from church on Sunday because I speak at retreats. One woman remarked to him, "I guess her career is more important than the church." Greg normally doesn't pass these comments on, because I tend to start rehearsing my clever retort in case this person ever makes the same comment to me!

But this time, he slipped and mentioned it. I laughed, which was such a different response that we both stared at each other and said nothing.

Over the next few days I took her comment to God during my times of quiet, asking, *What do I need to know about this?* Often, people's comments have opened a door to ways I need God's further transformation. As I laid her criticism before God day after day, I remembered how I had agonized over hit-and-run speaking engagements and wished for opportunities to build relationships, even short-lived ones. In all those times with God, I felt impressed to specialize in retreats to allow for interaction with people. I realized I'd laughed at the church member's comment because it didn't ring true. I'd already gotten my direction from God, and her opinion wasn't informed.

In solitude, I further asked God what I needed to know about this woman. It occurred to me that she wanted attention from me and didn't feel she was receiving it. So I began asking God how I might pay a healthy kind of attention to her.

"Without solitude," wrote Henri Nouwen, "we become victims of other people's opinions."[7] Part of my heart wants other people's approval, and so their criticisms sting. Unkind, thoughtless remarks send us brooding and steal passion from our purposes, but solitude gives us a place to inquire of the Lord about our place in "the family business." As we become confident of God's leading, it doesn't matter as much if others don't approve or fail to understand what we're doing.

Times of solitude help us quiet the traffic in our heads, allowing us to hear God and see our purposes more clearly. Daily periods of solitude provide margins of time throughout our day, so that every hour and minute isn't soaked up with activity. It's a relief to take a break in the backyard swing or to arrive early for an appointment and shut our eyes. "Spiritual persons...draw their life from a conversational relationship with God. They have 'a life beyond.'"[8] The "life beyond" provides clarity for the life here.

Solitude can also help us stay focused on our purposes. Christine Sine says, "Every Sunday, Tom and I take about an hour before church to journal. We look at last week and this week to discover what we want to accomplish and how we are going to allocate our time. Both of us want our lives to be more rooted in God. The only way to do that is to be intentional about changing our priorities." Journaling this way can help us consider the next step in our purposes and make time for it in our schedule. We move toward our purpose in small but important ways.

"Sometimes we think we can increase our effectiveness by becoming busier and busier, yet I think we need to get less busy and more focused on God," Christine continues. "When my husband, Tom, visited Mother Teresa's Sisters of Charity in Calcutta, who are well known for their work among the poor, he found they spent only five hours a day among the poor. The rest is spent in prayer, meditation, and things that focus them on God. Their effectiveness and ability to keep going is multiplied incredibly because of their time with God."

WAYS TO GET AWAY WITH GOD

You may be thinking, *But pursuing purpose in life will make me more busy. How will I ever find time to contemplate God?* The effort must be made because, as we move beyond our circle into the realm of God's purposes, we need regular solitude and getaways to establish a critical distance from our involvement. In that separate place we can ask, *Is what I do still appropriate? What needs to change?*

One way we can deliberately choose solitude with God is through personal retreats. Jesus, the paramount doer within Scripture, often took getaways. After feeding the five thousand, he ignored the perfect photo opportunity, pushing the disciples out to sea in a boat while he went off alone onto the mountain "by himself to pray. When evening came, he was there alone" (Matthew 14:22-23).

A more startling case is Jesus' response to the twenty-four-hour period described in Mark 1:29-35. Imagine how his Day-Timer organizer might have read:

DAY 1:

ACTION LIST	NOTES
Heal Peter's mother-in-law from a fever (verses 29-31).	Allow several hours. You can't be quick healing the relative of a friend.
Heal many sick people (verses 32, 34).	Allow time to listen to their stories and receive their thanks.
Cast demons out of many people (verses 32, 34).	Allow even more listening time!
Answer questions and interact with the "whole town gathered at the door" (verse 33).	How big is this town?
May have also happened on the same day: Preach authoritative, spell-binding message in the synagogue (verses 21-27).	Allow some downtime to catch a breath.

DAY 2:

ACTION LIST	NOTES
Go off to a solitary place to pray (verse 35).	Get started while it's still dark.

When I've heard this passage taught, it's been used to make listeners feel guilty that they don't get up early to pray even if the previous day was busy. It seems to me that the love relationship between Father and Son is forgotten when it's taught this way. Could it perhaps be true that Jesus got up early to pray not just to set us a good example, but because he longed to be with the Father? During Day 1, Jesus probably communicated with God all day long, but perhaps he yearned to spend a chunk of time alone with God. As he first began to awaken on Day 2, he saw an opportunity for quiet. Most mothers of young children have this experience—*Nobody's up yet. I'll grab some coffee and quiet!*

The interesting thing about Jesus' getaways in general, and this one in particular, is that he could not be contacted. Perhaps if he'd had a pager, he would have turned it off even though many of the previous day's formerly sick and demon-possessed people may have needed him. Jesus was the Messiah, but he did not have a "messiah complex," thinking the world couldn't get along without him. He left important work for other people to do. Yet you and I are unwilling to leave the telephone unanswered as we collect ourselves before God. Jesus knew his work was fueled by his love relationship with the Father, and he pursued that relationship even if it made him unavailable to do good things.

In the same way, we may need to spend a day or weekend alone at a retreat center. Clearing a day is difficult, but it's amazing how obstacles can disappear when we desire to be with God. As we make these a regular part of our lives, we'll serve out of our abundance instead of out of our essence.

Another way we can pursue solitude with God is through snatches of time. You may remember JoeAnn Ballard from chapter 6; she has served as a foster parent to fifty-five children and has directed Neighborhood Christian Centers in Tennessee and Mississippi, so you can imagine what her schedule looks like. When longer amounts of time aren't available, JoeAnn organizes her time to include the solitude she needs: "When Monroe [her husband] is out of town as he was yesterday and today, I stay up after everybody else has gone to bed and read the Bible and pray until 2 A.M. After we eat dinner on Sunday afternoons, I go to a special chair and spend three hours in prayer and study while everyone else naps. On the first three days of the month, donors and clients are out cashing their checks and paying bills so I am quiet in my office. My car doesn't need a radio. If I have thirty minutes to go somewhere, I think and pray." The interesting thing about JoeAnn's method is that it is so intentional. She doesn't just *happen* on the time to pray; she *looks* for it and even *designs* it.

It helps to have twenty minutes twice a day to "waste on the Lord, to sit like Mary at his feet while others are getting things done," says Trappist monk Basil Pennington. He talks about how people who do this don't lose time, but "they in fact get more done and with more peace and joy. Why? Because God has more freedom to work in their lives and they have more freedom to let God work. They are free to not get in God's way with all their own plans, imaginings, and fears."[9]

GOD IS EAGER TO MEET WITH US

When I first began experimenting with solitude, I found it uncomfortable because, to be honest, I didn't think God liked me very much. My conversations with other women led me to believe that I wasn't the only one who felt that being with God alone wasn't too exciting. Why? Part of it is that we're so conscious of our sin—especially those of us who sin a lot. Doesn't God get tired of us? Why would God speak to us? Yet he has a long track record of speaking to people, even those who make mistakes. We see God coming alongside Hagar, for example, in moments of doubt and despair. She had many reasons to doubt that her master's God would speak to her. She was not one of Abraham's people, but a darker-skinned foreigner. Hagar was a slave—and a rebellious one. When commanded to become a surrogate mother, she did so but then taunted Sarah, who mistreated her until she fled (Genesis 16:6).

God came to Hagar, a runaway slave woman for whom so many things had gone wrong. He didn't lecture her about her attitude. He told her that her son would not have to live in slavery as she had, but he would be a wild donkey of a man—free. Her son would make a success of the purpose others had chosen for her (to be a container for an embryo, mother to a castoff child). After God spoke these encouraging words to Hagar (Genesis 16:7-13), she said to the Lord: "You are the God who sees me" (verse 13).

Later, when her son's life and hers were threatened, God came to her again. This time, an angel saved them by providing a well of water. He also spoke tenderly to her, prophesying that her son would become a "great nation" and "God was with the boy" (Genesis 21:17-20). His career would be a success and he would know God; isn't that what most mothers want?

I love to imagine these hopeless-yet-God-infused scenes in Hagar's life. As a slave she had so few choices, and the one she had made (to taunt her mistress) cost her dearly. God spoke to her in the midst of her consequences, and instead of punishing her, he provided the well to save her life and to see her purpose fulfilled in Ishmael.

So often I've thought, *How can I expect to bond with God with the selfish attitude I have?* But God is eager to help me when I come to him and I say, "You see my faults. You love me. I surrender to you the things that trouble me—my friends, my work, my appalling sin." I regret having held back from him.

These intense times with God create a heart of love, and working from a heart of love is the secret to continuing passion and accomplishment. Vincent van Gogh, who knew love because he saw so little of it, wrote, "Whoever loves much performs much, and can accomplish much, and what is done in love is well done."[10] No matter how purposeful we are, skillful we may become, or successful others may say we are, nothing will ever outsatisfy the love and companionship with God that is always available to us.

QUESTIONS TO PONDER OR DISCUSS

1. Does a Saturday with nothing to do sound good? If you had one, what would you do? If you had six of them, what would you do? What would you be willing to give up to have a few of them?
2. How could you enjoy God's presence in the work you do now?

EXPERIMENT IN LISTENING PRAYER

Ask God, *What are some regular times I can look forward to being with you?*

BIBLE PASSAGE TO CONTEMPLATE

> My soul finds rest in God alone; my salvation comes from him (Psalm 62:1).

Meditate on the account of Hagar (Geneses 16:1-15), especially her words in verse 13:

> "You are the God who sees me," for she said, "I have now seen the One who sees me."

———

TEN

NOT ENOUGH CONFIDENCE...TOO MUCH CONFIDENCE

L aura told me that she was inspired during the weekend retreat in which I talked about pursuing our life purposes. She had come to realize that her concern about the challenges deaf people face stemmed from a God-given purpose to be a "voice to the voiceless." But she confessed she was also fearful. She said, "I'd love to take a class and learn sign language, but how can I be sure I can do it? If it gets tough I will be tempted to quit. I've never finished anything that has really helped anyone!"

I've met many women who share Laura's self-doubts. They think, *Someone with more education and energy could do a better job. I have the skills to partic- ipate in an inner-city mural project or sports program, but well...they just wouldn't want me. I don't have what it takes. If I step out with this new project or volun- teer in this different way, what will happen if it fails? Or worse, what if it suc- ceeds? What if people laugh at me or I lose my friends?*

As we begin to live our purposes in life, foundational issues of self present themselves over and over. We gain courage through exploring Scripture to see how God esteems people and through praying for God's help to see our- selves the way he sees us. As we read his Word, we need to ask, *What does God say about my worth and usefulness to him? How can I obey God's call on my life even when I feel fearful or lazy?*

Some might say we should wait to pursue purpose in life until we've got this worked out, but then we'd wait forever. It's an ongoing conflict, which is why even people who appear successful struggle with self-doubt. After you've been fulfilling what you believe God is calling you to do, expect that voice to knock on the door of your guts and say, *Not you!* Perhaps it isn't until we've stepped out for God that we realize how bankrupt we are of the confidence needed to do what we dream of doing. Becoming part of the family business will force us to examine these self-related issues over and over, and we work them out over and over as we move along.

It is difficult to keep pursuing purpose in life when we don't have a proven track record. In our heart of hearts, we may even doubt that we have any substantial value in this world. We mull over our failures and uncomfortable feelings, and when we add them up, we feel like a zero.

Confidence—at least a small seed of it—is necessary if we're to do what God has put in our hearts to do, yet most of the purposeful women I interviewed said they had little, if any. Why is that? Confidence is not something reserved for a chosen few. Confidence comes when we risk stepping out in faith and God doesn't fail us, so we try again and—wow, this great thing happens! The track record begins forming, but we're so conscious of how completely dependent we are on God that we still don't feel confident.

Elsie Purnell, who served with her husband, Herb, as a missionary in northern Thailand and also reared three children, now leads support groups for adult missionary kids. In spite of her many achievements, she tells of her continuing struggle with self-worth. "I am a phlegmatic. I have low blood pressure. I don't like challenges. Everything I do, I have to force myself to do. I take the step of faith, saying, 'God, I'm only doing this because you've asked me.' I have to make myself do things. Through different experiences, God has shown me he can use me and even speak through me. I was a nobody, but he showed me he could glorify himself through me.

"Once when I was the Sunday school superintendent at an expatriate church in Chaing Mai [Thailand], I worked on a committee with other women I looked up to. The others thought our retreat for the young girls should be done a certain way, but I felt strongly my idea was right. We were close friends so it took courage for me to insist. It was done as I suggested, and it turned out to be a turning point in the girls' lives—and mine. I realized God could speak through me to lead others. I wasn't necessarily proud. When God is in it, it has a humbling effect."

This "success" gave Elsie courage to try other things here and there, which is how confidence grows. As our confidence in God's willingness to use us grows, we need to be developing simultaneously a God-processed view of ourselves—learning it in our minds, absorbing it into our hearts, and trying it out in our behavior.

CORE TRUTHS THAT BUILD CONFIDENCE

We can also find confidence simply by learning more about how we are viewed by the God who has chosen us to pursue his purposes. Here are some truths to read, chew on, and explore.

You are near to the heart of God. We have value because God is absolutely near to us: "'Am I only a God nearby,' declares the LORD, 'and not a God far away?'" (Jeremiah 23:23). We are creatures with whom God has something to do, whom he created and loves and delights in: "The LORD your God is with you, he is mighty to save. He will take great delight in you, he will quiet you with his love, he will rejoice over you with singing" (Zephaniah 3:17). God lives within us and desires intimate fellowship with us. His eyes don't leave us and he sees a hopeful future in store for us: "'For I know the plans I have for you,' declares the LORD, 'plans to prosper you and not to harm you, plans to give you hope and a future'" (Jeremiah 29:11).

You are endowed with splendor. When I am tempted to believe I can be of little use to the kingdom, I must taste and see that I am of great worth to God. Says Ranelda Hunsicker, author of *The Hidden Price of Greatness*:

> The words of Isaiah 55:5 apply to all of God's children, not
> just Israel: "He has endowed you with splendor." But what if

I've failed? Lamentations 4:1-2 describes what happens to the splendor when we rebel against him: "How the gold has lost its luster, the fine gold become dull! The sacred gems are scattered at the head of every street. How the precious sons of Zion, once worth their weight in gold, are now considered as pots of clay, the work of a potter's hands!" But even in the dung heap, we still have worth divinely attributed to us. As Paul said in Romans 11:29, God's gifts are irrevocable.

You have a special purpose. As Henrietta Mears worked with Sunday school teachers, she urged them to instill in their students a sense of personal worth in God's kingdom: "They must feel that there is a task for them to do, that there is a place marked X for every person in God's kingdom. Here is my X; no one can stand on this place but me. Now I must help others to find their place. God has a job for every Christian, and no one else can fulfill it."[1]

Your "X" will look different from everyone else's because it grows out of your heritage, experiences, and inborn tendencies you may not even understand. Too often we look at others who present such a fine picture we assume that having a purpose would mean behaving as they do. But every purpose is homegrown and takes it own shape in the Potter's hands.

Certain circumstances may convince us we need to put our life purpose on hold, for example, singleness or being the mother of young children. Like Henrietta Mears in the past, Toni Baldwin served as a single woman on a church staff (recently as director of children's ministries and then family ministries). She talks about the reluctance single women feel in moving forward in what God is calling them to do. "In my early thirties, I felt like I was in a holding pattern. I didn't even buy dishes, because I thought that when I met the right man, I'd have a shower and pick out those things. I didn't realize I thought that way, but I did. Just as boys are raised to assert who they are, girls need to be told they're complete individuals whom God created with significant gifts to be used."

You have a responsibility to grow. The parable of the talents illustrates how we need to use what we've been given, not bury it because we're afraid we won't get it right (Matthew 25:14-30). "It is bad citizenship of the kingdom to waste our potential for usefulness," says author Kay Lindskoog. "Self-improvement is part of good citizenship. We have a responsibility to use our gifts and opportunities in life, but not to exploit them. We need to live with charity, integrity, and joy and keep increasing our understanding of ourselves and God."

As good stewards of ourselves, we take the time to assess our skills and strengths, which is often called "self-definition." Learning about spiritual gifts, temperament, learning styles, and so on shows us why we interact as we do with people, information, and the environment. Books such as *What Color Is Your Parachute?* can help us determine the orientation of our memory, natural abilities, powers of observation, reasoning, dexterity, strengths, and communication skills.

Acquiring "self-definition" isn't the same as "data collection." The data we collect to understand our purposes in life center on the question, "What breaks our hearts?" Self-definition, however, is about recognizing our abilities and skills, which helps us find appropriate tasks to fulfill our purposes. For example, my data collection has told me that I have a heart for the poor and oppressed, and I've loved volunteering weekly at the Samaritan Center so much that I considered applying for the position of assistant director. But my self-definition efforts confirm that I am an introvert, and as I prayed about taking on this new role, I could see myself hiding in the bathroom after the first week. So I continue to volunteer weekly and to enjoy writing about social justice issues—all alone in a quiet room! As an introvert, I understand my responsibility to develop people skills, but I also thank God for making me love words so I can work by myself.

Is this focusing on self appropriate? Self-knowledge is helpful and becomes a problem only when we become obsessed with self-improvement—reading only self-help books, taking an endless number of self-discovery quizzes, spending too much time in self-improvement classes. Our goal is never to become fascinated with self or to create a "better me," but to cooperate with God as he delights in watching the woman he created learn to walk, to run, to sprint.

The unnamed author of the ancient revered book *The Cloud of Unknowing* wrote: "Do not shrink from the sweat and toil involved in gaining real self-knowledge, for I am sure that when you have acquired it you will very soon come to an experiential knowledge of God's goodness and love."[2] The more we know about ourselves, the more we see the graciousness of God in forming us with strengths and redeeming our failures in projects, promises, and relationships. We may have blown it this time, but God will keep moving within us and do other exciting things through us.

JoeAnn Ballard, the founder of Neighborhood Christian Centers (mentioned already in chapters 6 and 9), tells how God moves through her frequent speaking engagements: "Getting up to speak is the most fearful situation you can put me in. That's not me. I have learned to say to God, *You have put me where I'm not capable*, and God says to me, *This is what you say first....Second, I'll help you remember*. It's a daily walk with the Lord."

Administrative work scares JoeAnn as well: "The other day I sat at my desk and said, *God, I'd like to rake this stuff off my desk and push it on the floor and never come back here again*. But he says, *I am with you—even to the ends of the earth*. The real me would have been a better factory worker."

JoeAnn illustrates how a sense of powerlessness can propel us into constant conversation with God. The path through fear involves holding on to the leader who draws us forward. We may never feel courageous, but we simply move forward with our purposes, knowing that fear is normal.

KEEPING OUR FOCUS ON GOD

In the moments we aren't stricken by the temptation to doubt ourselves, we can become charmed into secretly believing we know more than others and our way is right. When others criticize us, we can be tempted to set them straight about who we are and why our actions were appropriate (if not aloud, then in our minds, thinking, *There's only one way to run this grief group, and by golly, it's my way!*) Our culture tells us that if we're savvy women, we have to promote ourselves and become important in some arena. So we work hard to achieve a little status; no wonder no one wants to partner with us in our purposes.

Serving God requires death to self. Dying to self and coming alive to God allows me to admit my weaknesses. Because I am loved by God, I can confess my flaws—laziness, grouchiness, self-doubt—and trust God to keep on transforming me. I no longer need to appear perfect to friends, family, and anyone who attends my high-school reunion.

Dying to self also means embracing God day after day, saying, *I am the one you love. I am the one you died for. I am the one you called to jump on board your purposes.* The glory comes later, and by then I won't be starved for it anymore. In the meantime, I become less concerned about one-upping the people around me. I focus on God in the midst of a self-promoting culture and each day pledge not to forget the way of the burning heart.

Just as moments of self-doubt require us to focus on God's nearness, times of self-congratulation require us to focus on God's majesty and transcendence. Because God is supreme in power and unsurpassed in perfection, I see that I am only human and common sense says I need to surrender to God, who is so much greater than myself. Part of God's holiness is his otherness—that I am nothing like him and will find my hope only through a love relationship with this incomparable God.

This holy, majestic God cares about someone other than himself, and he calls me to do the same. While my culture tells me to serve myself, to focus on my needs, and to push myself forward, my God says to participate in the redemption of others: "Do nothing out of selfish ambition or vain conceit, but in humility consider others better than yourselves. Each of you should look not only to your own interests, but also to the interests of others" (Philippians 2:3-4).

Self-congratulation and self-doubt are both part of a bigger temptation: to be obsessed with *me.* In either case, my deliverance comes in absorbing into every fiber of myself the truth about God and the truth about me.

When I am tempted by self-doubt: I don't believe I can do anything. I fear that others are better equipped for the task at hand. But my fears are overcome when I remember key truths about God: He is absolutely near; he will never forsake me or leave me desolate; he delights in me and in molding me as his vessel. This knowledge also helps me grasp the truth about myself, that I am loved by God and he has endowed me with capacities and abilities. As a good steward, I need to let God use those things to bless others.

When I am tempted by self-congratulation: I believe I can do anything I put my mind to. I may even think I know more than others, especially my spouse or coworkers. I'm sure that if they'd listen to me, they'd do better. But the truths I encounter in my relationship with God remind me that I am not the center of the universe, just one member of humanity. God, the true center of the universe, is greater and more powerful than I can imagine, far beyond my capabilities and understanding. As I die to myself, I will find great meaning in God and he will use me for his service.

Even after we've worked through the above truths, the tendencies to focus on self often linger. We're certain that we're of little use to God or we overestimate our skill and importance. We will need to confront the temptations of self-obsession over and over. In the meantime, the passion of our broken hearts will push us to move beyond our circle into scary situations; it will give us a voice when we have none and keep us going when our strength is gone. That passion may even outshout the confidence of others. Yes, they're quoting statistics and trends, but we have listened to the heart of God and that gives us an unexplainable—and unassailable—sense of wisdom and maturity.

QUESTIONS TO PONDER OR DISCUSS

1. Which of the four core truths identified in this chapter is most difficult for you to believe, not just in your mind but deep down inside?

2. From the lists below, consider the characteristics of a culturally acceptable self-obsession (left column) versus God's radical command to die to ourselves (right column). Find the cultural characteristic that describes you and then read the corresponding biblical characteristic and circle it.

CHARACTERISTICS OF WHAT OUR CULTURE CALLS SELF-ESTEEM	CHARACTERISTICS OF BIBLICAL WORTH AND BEHAVIOR
• I believe I am okay (acceptable).	• I believe that as a human I am a "very good" part of God's creation.
• I make mistakes, but everyone does.	• I not only make mistakes, but I tend to sin whenever it's fun, convenient, or promotes my causes. Everyone has this human problem.
• When someone attacks me, I should defend myself.	• When someone attacks me, it is always appropriate to ask God to show me that person's heart and ask how I am a part of the redemptive process in that person's life. This tells me if it's appropriate to defend myself.
• I shouldn't say negative things about myself.	• I should confess my faults to God, and often to other people too.
• I have a right to promote myself, to make myself look as good as possible—for example on a résumé.	• I have a responsibility to be honest and candid about my abilities, but not to try to make myself look better than the other fellow. Saying critical things about myself to elicit praise is also self-promotion.
• I should quiet my inner critic.	• I should examine myself rigorously and ask God to show me my character flaws. I shouldn't let my inner critic (the enemy's tool) take control and cause despair.
• I should be careful to take care of my own needs.	• I should consider my needs, but also the needs of others, and so far as it is possible, be eager to meet the needs of those around me.

EXPERIMENT IN LISTENING PRAYER

Ponder this prayer:

> God has created me to do him some definite service.
> He has committed some work to me which he has not
>   committed to another.
> I have my mission.
> I may never know it in this life
> But I shall be told it in the next.
> I am a link in a chain.
> A bond of connection between persons
> He has not created me for naught
> I shall do good—I shall do his work
> I shall be an angel of peace
> A preacher of truth in my own place
> While not intending it.
> If I do but keep his commandments.[3]
>
> —John Henry Newman

BIBLE PASSAGE TO CONTEMPLATE

He has endowed you with splendor. (Isaiah 55:5)

How the gold has lost its luster, the fine gold become dull! The sacred gems are scattered at the head of every street. How the precious sons of Zion, once worth their weight in gold, are now considered as pots of clay, the work of a potter's hands! (Lamentations 4:1-2)

ELEVEN

NURTURING GOD-EMPOWERED PASSION

What if you have an idea of what your purpose is, but you have no energy to get out of the chair and do anything more about it? You know God's heart is broken and so is yours, but it all sounds too scary, too uncomfortable, or like too much work! Besides, it sounded more heartbreaking when the eloquent speaker described the cause than it does now that you're home, nestled in front of the television.

For some reason you lack—or have squelched—passion. Maybe you wish the steps to fulfill your purposes came in a shrink-wrapped kit labeled "Steps 1, 2, and 3" with all the information you need. Instead, those steps involve making difficult phone calls, writing introductory letters, creating a business plan, or seeking a grant. Some of these challenges are downright scary.

Or maybe you lack passion because you see it as a negative quality. A friend in her thirties has a similar negative reaction when women talk about having a passion for what God is calling them to do. "For people my age," she said, "passion reminds us of parents who went through the 1960s search for self. Passion makes you irresponsible and unreliable. We've avoided it because we've seen it hurt people and break up families."

Or perhaps you think passionate people alienate others. After all, Scarlett O'Hara saved Tara and never went hungry again, but so what? Nobody liked her, and the man in her life, frankly, got sick of this self-centered woman and walked out.

These points are well taken. Passion traditionally has a caution-to-the-wind sexual connotation as well as a sense of self-will and being driven. Other times it's laced with so much idealism it's no earthly good, and we've all been turned off by those whose passion is overbearing. But when it's directed toward our God-given biblical purposes, passion means having a heart for someone or something, such as when Jesus cleansed the temple, quoting the psalmist: "Zeal for your house will consume me" (John 2:17; Psalm 69:9). Look at how Nehemiah described his burning passion to restore Jerusalem by helping rebuild its walls: "I had not told anyone what my God had put in my heart to do for Jerusalem" (Nehemiah 2:12). His downward career move from influential politician to governor of the untamed west was both his idea and God's idea. When God's people have lacked desire and diligence, God has urged his servants to be passionate.

From this perspective, passion is the capacity and willingness to care about the purposes God has burned into our hearts. We see hurts and dilemmas others don't see. We have an energy to do something about it when others don't. When others say, *I don't see anything wrong,* we're frustrated, thinking, *How can they say that? Someone has to* do *something.*

A healthy sense of passion propels us forward in our purposes—and for that reason healthy passion must be nourished. Without passion we lack energy, and so time slips away and our purposes fade. But if we choose to allow God to shape us into wise, passionate women, we'll be able to take the risks necessary to do what God has put in our hearts to do—and still keep our friends!

The New Testament figure Priscilla had this kind of passion. She was forced from her home in Rome when the emperor expelled all the Jews from the city. The first time we hear of Priscilla, she is living with her husband, Aquila, as a refugee in Corinth. In her place, I would want to find a new home quickly and settle there for the rest of my life. If Priscilla felt that way, she gave up her dream when she and Aquila met Paul, took him into their home, and worked closely with him in the church. Somehow this displaced woman tore herself from home after home as she moved to Syria, Ephesus, back to Rome, and then back to Ephesus. In each place she welcomed others, becoming a leader in the church, holding church in her home, and explaining the gospel more fully to people (Acts 18:2-3,18-19,26; Romans 16:3-5; 1 Corinthians 16:19; 2 Timothy 4:19).

Why would this refugee woman—a stranger and foreigner—give up her home to teach a religion soon to be declared illegal? She (with her husband-partner, Aquila) seems to have caught a vision for the "family business" purpose of converting the first-century world to Christ. Their personal mission involved fulfilling this task one town at a time. This passion for evangelism would explain how Priscilla adapted so well to being a stranger in each community and welcoming locals to a foreign faith. She seems to have taken the pain of being a constant newcomer and turned it into a ministry of bringing others in and welcoming them to God.

DEVELOPING RISK-TAKING SKILLS

Often the burning desire of our hearts will bring us to the brink of risk. In those moments, we (like Priscilla) will have to embrace at least a little of what risk-takers are known for: loving change, uncertainty, variety, intensity, unpredictability, flexibility, minimal structure, and perhaps even high conflict. Some people seem to be born with a natural desire to take risks, says Frank Farley, a psychologist at Temple University in Philadelphia. The challenge for those of us who aren't natural-born risk-takers is to embrace the level of change, uncertainty, and unpredictability needed to follow our God-given purposes in life.

In her book *To Build the Life You Want, Create the Work You Love,* author Marsha Sinetar lists the skills risk-takers need in a helpful chart, "A Step Ladder of Risk-Taking Skills."[1] Here are a few of the "superior risk-taking skills" she lists and how they relate to purpose in life.

High tolerance for ambiguity. Can you live without knowing exactly what's going on? Can you pray and wait? And wait? Have you tried to view situations with God's penetrating vision to see what doors are open? An ability to function when we don't know what's going on involves managing our feelings and deciding which ones to pay attention to at the moment.

It's important to remember that fear is normal. Yes, I'm afraid to take a missions trip or to be trained as a divorce mediator, but if I weren't afraid, *that* would be unusual. Instead of dwelling on my limitations, I focus on the next step in my purpose-related task—cook this turkey, fill out the form, greet this student. When I feel like quitting, I do the next two little tasks required. Gradually, I let go of my fear. This do-what-is-in-front-of-you technique works well for me because I slowly become absorbed in the purpose of it all, and my interest increases so that it outweighs the fear. (Sometimes unappealing tasks signal a need for change, but that decision is better made from a distance than when we're launching the task.) Like the servants who were faithful with five and two talents and were given more (Matthew 25:20-23), we become faithful in small things—writing that letter, showing up to volunteer, reading the want ads—then God brings larger tasks our way. The success of the smaller steps creates momentum to tackle the larger ones.

My tolerance for ambiguity has increased since I've come to realize that it's not my job to solve other people's problems. In each task, I'm called to pray and watch as God does the solving. For example, as I volunteer at the Samaritan Center, I have fun tending the shower desk and exchanging quips with clients while helping them find jeans that fit. My "deep gladness" of purpose flows not from getting clients successfully settled in a place of their own or helping them become the kind of people who do settle down; my joy comes through the process of partnering with God. When a client can find and maintain a regular place to live, I am thrilled, but partnering with God gives life a greater sense of meaning than the activity itself ever could. As I serve, my main business is to pray for clients and co-workers while we interact. If the director is late and the rest of us sit out front waiting in the cold, my service is not wasted. It is meaningful because I have still partnered with God, interacting with clients and praying for them as we talk. I am delighted to be on board. This "deep gladness" to which Frederick Buechner refers exudes from the self-forgetfulness of being involved in the family business—working out God's purposes on this earth.

Transcends "good" or "bad" polarizations. Can you accept the mature and immature qualities of the director of the program in which you're involved? Can you have a heart for someone even though you disapprove of his or her behavior? At the Samaritan Center one morning I helped a young woman fill out some forms. Her baby had been placed in foster care because this young woman was homeless, so she was completing forms to keep the baby from being adopted. She believed she'd get on her feet someday. Was the choice to prevent the adoption good or bad? I agonized inside. On the one hand, I wanted her baby to be adopted so he wouldn't have to live on the streets. But I also saw this young woman's heart—how could I look at this mother and want her child taken from her? There are few easy answers or simple solutions, but I have been called to this situation not to judge this woman or to solve her problems, but to walk alongside her, meeting her needs, helping her spell four-syllable words.

Correctly gauges probability of outcomes. A study of personalities and temperaments can help you know what to expect from people, just as various experiences help us know what is likely to happen in a given situation. Still, people are so unpredictable that I frequently use these two self-protective questions to analyze risks:

1. *If I risk, what would be the worst that could happen?*

If the worst is that I'll embarrass myself or be afraid, is that so bad? If the worst is that I could damage someone else, how can I eliminate that factor? How much money or time could this cost me?

2. *How much regret will I feel if I pass this up?*

If I will always look back and wish I'd done it, I don't pass it up. My friend was asked to write a book with one of her heroes, but the project didn't pay a great deal and would take too much time. The logical answer was no. "But," I asked her, "will you look back and wish you'd done it?"

"Definitely," she said. "This is a golden opportunity to learn what I need to know from this wise person." My friend accepted the assignment and barely survived financially, but she is glad she took the risk. "No college course could have taught me as much or given me such contacts," she says.

Sinetar cautions against confusing superior risk-taking skills with impulsivity. We want to become wise risk-takers, not daredevils. Here are a few other risk-taking skills Marsha Sinetar lists to describe *wise* risk-takers:

- floats "trial balloons"
- investigates long-range probabilities
- excellent improviser, thinks on feet, trusts instincts
- manages fear and indecision
- can say no to short-term gain to win long-term advantage
- takes high risks after close scrutiny of variables or consequences
- tolerates delays
- uses errors as feedback
- keeps playing with solutions
- prefers own answers yet remains open to input, a natural "explorer"

We don't all have these skills, but we know people who do. We can lay our decisions before them and ask their advice. When we attend conferences or find ourselves in networking situations, we can look for people who have these attitudes and allow their risk-taking skills to recharge us and release our passion.

According to Sinetar, those with below-average risk-taking skills have these tendencies:

- easily distracted, unfocused, or confused
- thinks in details, misses big picture
- overthinks and overtalks goals as a way of eliciting "don't do it" advice from others
- wants guaranteed outcome and advice
- fears trying or hearing new ideas
- easily discouraged, finds delays depressing
- passes the buck, avoids accountability, blames the advice-giver when things go wrong
- needs dominant experts, authority figures to give how-to advice

Psychological studies show that many women are slow to take risks, but one factor that helps them to do so is the feeling that they are on secure ground. "When women are very certain, they are more willing to go out on a limb."[2] What makes uncertain ground secure? In her research on female entrepreneurs, Joanne Wilkens found that familiar experiences, relationships, surroundings, and location can give women the confidence, insight, and knowledge necessary for risk-taking behavior. For example, three-fourths of women who started their own business had a parent, grandparent, or close relative who owned a business.[3] When you need to take a risk, bring in a familiar element—volunteer with a friend, teach from a familiar Bible book, serve in a location that is familiar or somehow fascinating to you.

LETTING GOD SPEAK TO YOU

Perhaps you're convinced that risk taking requires too many skills you don't have. Nurture your passion by bringing this normal feeling to God in conversation. JoeAnn Ballard, who you may remember comes alongside others as a foster mother and organizer of Neighborhood Christian Centers, finds courage in conversations with God.

"The natural JoeAnn is fearful and wouldn't like to be involved in ministry at the level I am," she says. "I don't like confrontations—even though I have them all the time. If a person read what I wrote in the raw, they would make fun of it. The real me wants to walk away. Sometimes I'm left alone with a task that's too much for me and I say to God, *I'll fall on my face if you don't deliver me.* God's saying to me, *I'm with you. Try it. Go ahead. This is what I want to get accomplished.*"

What is the result? "I'm a stone God can throw any way he wants to throw," says JoeAnn.

No doubt one source of JoeAnn's quiet but steady energy is the pain of her past. As a foster child, a minority, and a grade-school student without a textbook, she has gone on to help children, become a community leader, graduate from college, and receive an honorary doctorate degree for her achievements. Like her, the pain of your past may be a good source of energy to move you forward in your purpose. As you find wholeness and healing, retain your broken heart about your past pain. Recycle it so that the healing you receive from God will nurture a passion to serve others. I've met several women who have worked through bulimia and who now help young girls and their parents do the same. They take the comfort they received from the "Father of compassion and the God of all comfort" and use it to comfort others with the "comfort we ourselves have received from God" (2 Corinthians 1:3-4).

Whether it's through our hurt or our fear, partnership with God fuels our passion to go on. Amy Carmichael, a single woman missionary to India, founded a community known as the Sisters of the Common Life. She is well known for her thirty-five books detailing her more than fifty years in India, where she worked with children, rescuing girls from temple prostitution and establishing a home and school for them.[4] Here is an example of one of her many pivotal conversations with God:

> On this day many years ago I went away alone to a cave in
> the mountain called Arima. I had feelings of fear about the
> future. I went there to be alone with God. The devil kept
> on whispering, "It is all right now, but what about after-
> wards? You are going to be very lonely." And he painted
> pictures of loneliness—I can see them still. And I turned to
> my God in desperation and said, "Lord, what can I do?
> How can I go on to the end?" And he said, "None of them
> that trust in Me shall be desolate." That word has been
> with me ever since.[5]

There's just something about stepping out that seems overwhelmingly scary or difficult, but passion for our purpose can grow as we stay connected with God. About four years ago, I was working on one of my regular assignments to write Bible study curriculum for adults. At my own request, I'd been assigned a passage based on my life purpose of social justice. As I planned a session on Matthew 25:31-46, I became so grieved I couldn't write another word. *Where have I seen a hungry person and ignored her?* I agonized. *Who has been naked, and I've left her standing that way? Where have I overlooked a stranger?* Sure I was helping others see God's plan for loving the poor and oppressed, but I was no longer involved in a regular, ongoing ministry to the poor. I sat at my desk and explained to God how I'd found no opportunities in our new location. (New? We'd lived there for five years.) As I offered these reasons for not living out one of my stated purposes in life, I laid my head on my desktop and pleaded with God to let me off the hook because of my cramped schedule. *I write about social justice issues. Isn't that enough?* All I could hear was Jesus saying to me, *Don't you recognize me in the faces of the "least of these my brethren" on your street corner? In the news?* Finally, I did what I've never done before or since—I shut off my computer during a workday and began making personal telephone calls. After several calls, I found out that a drop-in center was starting up, but I would have to take off work to volunteer. Never!

I put my head down on my desk again and asked God to speak to me. I saw the face of my friend, Barbara Gage, whom I've met with in the early morning for years even though I hate to get up in the morning. *Could I volunteer early before work?* I called the drop-in center's director again, gulped hard, and offered to come in early. Yes, they would open on Mondays at 7 A.M. if I would show up. Handing out towels and listening to clients' jokes now has become an integral part of my life, but I almost tuned God out. Through years of training in solitude and meditation, I've come to recognize the voice of God—ever present, all-seeing within me—speaking to my soul in an otherwise ordinary work day. I know I can trust God, my insightful Parent, to help me live out my purposes in a doable way.

Volunteering at the Samaritan Center has come to feel like "holy business" because it's not about me. It's not even about the clients and coworkers I've come to love. It's about God. On my own, I would never do it. God has drawn me into this, and he keeps placing drops of mercy within me and reminding me that he is the longtime defender of the poor and oppressed (Psalm 10:12-18). I'm the newcomer. As I ask God to make my heart like his, he continues to remind me of his passion and purposes. He whispers, *Try to get excited with me, Jan.* The more willing I am to follow his purposes for my life, the more passionate about them I become. God fuels my passion and gives me the courage I need to risk.

CHARACTER REGULATES PASSION

Perhaps you're full of energy and passion, eagerly serving God. Perhaps the bookstore owner saw you coming and hid this book, but you found it anyway. Maybe you've been hearing warning signals in your head for years: *Try to tone down. Passion is not a good thing.*

If you have a burning heart, you will at times find yourself wanting to penetrate the numbness and self-deception of people—even God's people—but you'll still want friends. How can you do that?

Check your heart continually. Fight self-righteousness by clinging to the heart of God. What sort of person is God calling you to be? How is God asking you to behave in order to have a heart for him alone? Don't ask, *Why isn't everyone else working as hard as I am?* There can be no room for grandiosity or lifting up self. Too often passionate Christians rant and rave and repeat themselves. It's better to present our purposes briefly in light of the doubts and failures we've experienced.

Offer hope. Too many passionate people are negative doomsayers. The prophet has a twofold role: to clarify what is wrong and to offer hope for making it right.[6] Elijah didn't just point out the wickedness of Ahab and Jezebel; he constantly urged them to repent and do what was right. Our message is, Here's what wrong, and here's what God's purposes tell us to do about it.

In medieval times, women had almost no voice, yet Catherine of Siena (1347–80) attempted to reform the church of her day. She had already attracted followers because of the holiness of her life, and she had aided people dying from the Black Plague as it swept Europe. "Drawn into the sociopolitical conflicts of the Italian city-states and the institutional chaos of that century's papacy, Catherine began to be a counselor and peacemaker. Sometimes successful in her efforts, sometimes betrayed by her unscrupulous allies, she worked vigilantly to reform what she considered to be the great scandal of Christendom: the decadence of the clergy and the flight of the papacy from Rome."[7] (She felt that by being stationed in Avignon, the pope would be unduly influenced politically by France's nobility. History agrees with her.) Can you identify with this woman who pleaded for honest pastors and church leaders to keep their hearts free from bribes?

But Catherine offered hope as well as admonition. Her extensive correspondence shows that "her bold denunciations could never be construed to signify disloyalty to the church. Her scathing indictments were accompanied by affirmations of love and concern."[8]

Offer clarity. As a prophet, Jesus excelled at coming up with a third option when only two were on the table. When the Pharisees tried to trick him about paying taxes, "Is it right to pay taxes to Caesar or not?" (Matthew 22:17-21), Jesus offered a third choice: Be fair to everyone; pay your taxes and give your money to God. It was so simple, yet so revolutionary. When a dispute arises, ponder what the real problem is and ask God to reveal what you and others need to know. Then offer that clarity in a humble spirit.

Major in the majors. Try to stay focused on the big picture. Sometimes I observe volunteers at the Samaritan Center standing around and talking about their cruise vacations in front of people without homes! This puts me on my high horse, but the Holy Spirit has nudged me to hold my tongue and not comment on it. At least they volunteer. It's better to save my input for bigger issues, such as the training process for volunteers.

You may dislike many details of a specific program, but it's better to let go of the smaller disputes and cash in on the bigger ones. If you're known as a whiner, who will listen to you? And if it's important to be listened to, remember that your kind and caring character speaks more loudly than your clever opinions.

Serve without self-consciousness. It's hard to do a good deed these days without wondering how it would look in a TV movie or on videotape. Somehow we have to rid ourselves of self-obsession and serve from the heart. The Good Samaritan character that Jesus dreamed up was "good" also in this sense. First, he quietly did what needed to be done. We, on the other hand, make a project out of everything. Our service isn't valid unless we solve all of a person's problems, fix the entire situation, and invite TV cameras to film it. Assuming we had stopped to take an interest in the wounded traveler in Jesus' story, we wouldn't have been satisfied until we held a press conference to launch a Jerusalem-to-Jericho traveler safety program.

Also, the Samaritan's approach was simple. He used the resources at hand. If a church group from today had come along, we might have voted on whether it was a good idea to give that innkeeper too much money, as the Samaritan did. What if some of it were wasted? And we'd have to come back a week later and hold a fund-raiser to pay for any future expenses. The Samaritan simply did what needed to be done—tending the wounds, lifting the broken man onto the donkey, arranging for the stay without haggling over money, and paying the additional expenses himself. The intriguing part of this shocking story about an enemy's saving an enemy is that the Samaritan was so uncalculating. May we follow his example.

Love your opponents. Catherine of Siena had a heart of love for those she wished to reform. A later pope said of her, "None ever approached her without going away better."[9] Some of us "reformers" destroy others by gossiping and focusing on our opponents' failings. We do well to remember that those with whom we disagree or who criticize our cause are people whom God loves, souls dear to his heart. When we follow in the footsteps of Jesus, who challenged the rich young ruler to give up his possessions, we'll take note that he presented the challenge only after he "looked at him and loved him" (Mark 10:21).

The space between God and another person is holy space. It is not space you and I are invited to enter in order to judge others for God. We respect that space by speaking truth in a general sense and praying God will speak the specific truth to that person.

Don't take yourself too seriously. Prophets can be serious, grumpy people. Shakespeare's leading lady in *The Merchant of Venice,* Portia, showed us how to be a gracious crusader as she set out to save her man from the meanspirited Shylock. Her soon-to-be husband had agreed to pay his friend's debt but, unexpectedly, could not. As a result, he was required to pay Shylock a pound of flesh. When Shylock insisted on payment, Portia pled the case, offering this legal loophole: The contract did not allow Shylock to spill a drop of blood.

How could he acquire a pound of flesh without a drop of blood? But before wise Portia offered this clever insight, she played peacemaker and reconciler. She appealed to Shylock to be merciful (much like Abigail with David), but he refused. He felt the consequence of his arrogance when she won. Wise Portia had everyone's best interest at heart, even that of her enemy, Shylock.

The amusing part of Portia's story, however, is how she pled her case—disguised as a male attorney. Neither her husband-to-be nor his friend knew until later that she was the one who rescued them. In so doing she avoided the Lady Bountiful trap. May those of us with great passion be this generous and gracious.

ROOTED IN GOD

Whether our challenge is to grow our passion or to keep it in balance, what saves us from ourselves is what always saves us: a vital relationship with God. When not concerned about knowing God or his purposes, we can become self-absorbed and unconcerned about the needs of others. And when passion is not rooted in a relationship with God, it can estrange us from the people we love and work with as we leave them out, look down on them, or run over them. Being passionate about a purpose in life makes no difference in this world without the security of God's love reminding us how desperately we need his grace.

"The recovery of passion begins with the recovery of my true self as the beloved," writes Brennan Manning. "If I find Christ I will find myself and if I find my true self I will find Him."[10]

QUESTIONS TO PONDER AND DISCUSS

1. Consider the risks you need to take to fulfill your purpose. What familiar footings could you provide so the risk wouldn't be as scary (familiar locations, people, relationships)?
2. In what situations in life have you taken risks (personal or professional) that turned out positively? What did you learn from them?
3. What was your last hunch, and how did it work out?

EXPERIMENT IN LISTENING PRAYER

Ask God, *What is it that I am most afraid of risking?*

BIBLE PASSAGE TO CONTEMPLATE

God is our refuge and strength,
    an ever-present help in trouble.
Therefore we will not fear, though the earth give way
    and the mountains fall into the heart of the sea,
though its waters roar and foam
    and the mountains quake with their surging.
There is a river whose streams make glad the city of God,
    the holy place where the Most High dwells....
"Be still, and know that I am God;
    I will be exalted among the nations,
    I will be exalted in the earth."
The LORD Almighty is with us;
    the God of Jacob is our fortress. (Psalm 46:1-4,10-11)

TWELVE

EVEN THE LONE RANGER HAD A SIDEKICK

W e can't follow our purpose and be a "Lone Ranger," because God's purposes are about people. Solitude feeds the soul, but so does community. Relationships with others round us out and teach us to partner with God and serve others. When purpose-full people are left to themselves, they can easily become narrow-minded, self-righteous know-it-alls. Isolating one's self from community or forming surface-only relationships deprives us of the nurturing, shaping hands of God provided through other people.

The word *relationship* doesn't appear in the Bible, but it's evidenced everywhere. God sent his Son to form a relationship with people because commandments printed on blocks of stone were not enough to transform our character and feed our soul. And they never will be. Confidence, know-how, and healing grow out of healthy relationships in which we lock arms, trust each other, and earn the right to say things that might otherwise seem too personal.

The necessary courage for risk taking and vision seeking is often nurtured by those who love and support us. Would Ruth have left her homeland and gone to live as a foreigner in Israel without Naomi? Would Esther have stood up to the king without her cousin Mordecai? How would Mary have fared without the encouragement of her older cousin, Elizabeth? Would Mary Magdalene have faced the guards at Jesus' tomb without her female companions? These women risked everything with the support of people they loved.

Living a purpose-full life can be lonely if others feel threatened by your pursuit of your God-given dream. They may feel snubbed that, since you began volunteering at a missions office, you don't have time to take long lunches. Or they may find your passion uncomfortable. A woman I met at a writer's conference told me that, as she began writing, a friend of hers made fun of the briefcase lying on the backseat of her car. "Are you trying to look important now?" she asked. "No," the woman told me. "I bought the brief-case to keep toddler goo off my manuscript."

Perhaps you've longed for connection and appreciation, as did Vincent van Gogh:

> There may be a great fire in our soul, yet no one ever comes
> to warm himself at it, and the passersby only see a wisp of
> smoke coming through the chimney, and go along their way.
> Must one tend the inner fire, have salt in oneself, wait
> patiently yet with how much impatience for the hour when
> somebody will come and sit down—maybe to stay? Let him
> who believes in God wait for the hour that will come sooner
> or later.[1]

Those who are willing to sit at my fire are the partners God gives me. I am honored to sit at their fire as well and nurture them, listen to them, and ponder what God is doing in them.

Women especially need the encouragement that partners in purpose can bring. "Psychologists have made significant discoveries regarding the impor-tance of relationships in women's lives," writes author Carol Gilligan. "According to these researchers, women identify themselves in terms of their relationships and make ethical decisions based on how their actions affect the people around them. Women seek to create a continually expanding web of connections and feel most comfortable when they are at the center of this web, surrounded by family, friends, and coworkers."[2]

God uses relationships to advance the kingdom, to teach mercy and justice, to help us hear the whimper of voiceless people. When you consider all the weighty, consequential things Jesus could have done in three short years of ministry, it's surprising how much time he spent on friendship, forming an inner circle of three: Peter, James, and John. At the most dramatic moment of his flesh-and-blood life, when he could have called ten thousand angels to help, Jesus asked these three to come alongside him. To do some practical tasks? No. "He took Peter, James and John along with him, and he began to be deeply distressed and troubled. 'My soul is overwhelmed with sorrow to the point of death,' he said to them. 'Stay here and keep watch'" (Mark 14:33-34).

We need friends, family, coworkers, and all sorts of partners in ministry to "stay here and keep watch," and we're called to do the same for them. We don't always have to give wise and wonderful advice, but we do need to sit at their fire, praying that they will know Christ and make him known.

PEOPLE WHO MAKE GOOD PARTNERS

Who are the kinds of people we should seek to populate the circle around our fire?

Influencers. Because of Miriam Adeney's unquenchable desire to connect with the world's cultures, she directs a program that helps Christians in Asia, Africa, and Latin America write books that are significant, biblically rich, and culturally contextualized in the language of their people. "This program cuts against the grain because it's not as financially productive as translating well-known American books," says Miriam. "But American books about child raising often aren't appropriate to another culture. Western theological books miss big issues in other cultures, such as poverty, oppression, interpretation of dreams, witchcraft, extended families, and elements of their indigenous religion."

So how does Miriam find the passion to swim upstream as she directs this challenging program? She talks about Gladys Jasper, an influencer in her life who managed a publishing firm in Asia, where Miriam lived in her twenties. "A lot of what motivates me today are the Gladys Jasper scripts I hear in my head. I absorbed this philosophy from her. I would not do this work if Gladys had not believed in this concept."

Meeting people in story. Reading biographies and bonding with fictional characters can keep us focused as well. When I first read Willa Cather's novel *O Pioneers!* I was impressed with how she spoke of the open land of the American West giving drive and purpose. This "unexplored territory" wrapped itself around the heart of the main character, Alexandra Bergson, as it had her father, Carl. When he died, she became the force behind building a farm and a semblance of civilization in a "wild land."

Others living on the Nebraska "divide," including her brothers, did not have Alexandra's pioneer spirit. Wrote Cather, "A pioneer should have imagination, should be able to enjoy the idea of things more than the things themselves."[3] Willa Cather's character, Alexandra (as well as Jane in *Jane Eyre*, Elizabeth Bennet in *Pride and Prejudice*, Celie in *The Color Purple*, the unnamed Mrs. de Winter in *Rebecca*, Jo March in *Little Women, Little Men*, and *Jo's Boys*), spurs me on with courage. She shows me that each of us has "unexplored territory" that somehow fascinates us as it does not others, and we move forward even when others misunderstand.

Family members. Mothers and daughters, sisters, and spouses have long partnered with one another in purpose. For example, Johanna Bethune was joined by her mother, Isabella Graham, in igniting and leading the American Sunday school movement.[4]

Sandy Burgess, a thirtyish stay-at-home mom who also does marketing and research for a Christian organization ten hours a week, cites her mother, Jane Nowlin, as a primary influencer. "She has always believed God had something for me to do. She's served in many positions but she says now is her time to support me. She and my husband are my day-by-day touchstones. If something in my interactions with people seems odd, I'll ask my mother's opinion. If I were on my own, I would spiral down toward analysis paralysis."

Parachurch organizations. Many women have found partners for their purpose while serving in a missions agency or community-based Bible study. Sandy Burgess has found another partner in the president of the parachurch organization for which she works, Women's Ministries Institute (WMI) in Pasadena, California. Through a convention in Spokane, Washington, Sandy met Pat Clary, president of WMI. They talked that week and kept in contact. "During the times I've felt no one has thought I've been capable of things, Pat has asked me to do something or confirmed God had a plan. Being involved in WMI has raised my eyes to other role models and raised my level of thinking. When I come home from a Women's Ministry symposium, I feel refreshed and fed even though I've worked hard, because I've been surrounded by godly women leaders. Then I can go back to what is before me."

Mentors, disciplers, and spiritual directors. By partnering with mentors, we can learn specific tasks, such as developing our devotional life, learning ministry skills, or working out the quirks of parenting or hospitality. Or we may need to be discipled, which usually involves learning the basics of Bible study, prayer, witnessing, and worship. A spiritual director partners with you by meeting regularly with you to ask, "Where is God in what you're doing? What is God leading you to do?" or "What is God saying to you these days?" Any of these partners may also work with you to develop a mission statement.

Besides these relationships, it's wise to be involved in one in which you are a giver: "Freely you have received, freely give" (Matthew 10:8). I always need someone who is shepherding me and someone I am shepherding. Those I mentor and direct challenge me and question me because they think I know the answers—which I don't. As a result, I seek God in new ways.

Many young women with leadership skills have burned out because of lack of direction. Sometimes they give up on the church and Christian circles because they don't receive the guidance they need to acquire skills and character. These things are best learned in relationships with women who sense our potential and help us nurture it.

No matter what our purpose, we will fulfill it better if we partner with someone or serve on a team. We can give each other feedback, offer encouragement when we're discouraged, and celebrate when things go well. Team members, both positive and negative, help us. Sandy Burgess describes it this way: "A woman will encounter various leaders who help her. She will meet people like Saul who take swipes at her; people like Peter who are leaders of great movements that she can learn from but won't have a lot of personal input into her life; people like Paul who are leaders with great passion but who don't have a lot of patience for people; people like Barnabas who act redemptively, helping her be useful for God's service even when she makes mistakes. Each of those leaders serves a purpose.

"Someone told me once, 'David had to serve under Saul to learn what he needed to know.' If nothing else, the 'Sauls' teach us to duck, which is better than putting up our fists." (See 1 Samuel 19:10.)

THE ART OF PARTNER-STYLE FRIENDSHIP

Friendships in which women view each others as partners in service have a unique dimension. When Henrietta Mears took over the college department at Hollywood Presbyterian Church, she met a woman named Mother Atwater, who had been the department superintendent.

> Miss Mears and Mother Atwater became close friends and Teacher (as Ms. Mears was called) leaned on this saintly woman for encouragement, especially for prayer. Miss Mears would frequently phone her concerning some urgent spiritual need and ask her to intercede. Besides prayer, the two of them spent every Thursday afternoon calling on students and winning them to Christ. Mother Atwater was on her knees at five every Sunday morning, praying for two hours or so for Miss Mears and the college department. Her ministry continued throughout Miss Mears' thirty-five years at the church, and the two of them died within a year of each other.[5]

This sort of friendship goes beyond the normal, helpful conversations about where to find what you need on sale or how to get kids to do their homework. It involves walking alongside someone, listening to another woman, forging a union of minds, persevering together, and being transparent. These friendships nurture our passion. In such friendships, people listen to each other, making observations and asking questions such as these:

- What is God calling you to do?
- What are your hopes, your deepest desires?
- Have you noticed how much you talk about this purpose?
- How are you managing your purposes in regard to family and work?
- What are your motives? Do they honor God?

In an increasingly mobile society in which dear friends often move away, we need to go out of our way to make the kind of friends to whom we can admit our faults. Feeling quite lonely after a recent move, I searched earnestly for women friends who had a heart for God's kingdom. I guessed Barbara Gage to be such a woman, and I pestered her to get together until she suggested we meet for breakfast. *Meet for breakfast?* I was shocked. I didn't know anyone ever had conversation over breakfast. I thought breakfast was what you carried with you from room to room as you tried to remember your name. As much as I hated the idea, I agreed to meet her at 6:00 A.M., laying out my clothes the night before on the floor (chalk line, crime scene-style) so I could slide out the door the next morning. I survived that first breakfast, and we have continued to meet for years. Relationships such as this one have been a formative part of my knowing God and seeking his purposes in my life.

From that experience, I learned the importance of going to great lengths for friendship. Relationships are so important that I am willing to be inconvenienced and reintroduce myself a few times without (too much) embarrassment. I understand better why Jesus did what our mothers taught us never to do: He invited himself over to Zaccheus's home (Luke 19:2-10). I now see the value of serving on committees and working at conferences (which I used to think took up too much time), because there I've found women who have become God-given pieces of my puzzle.

In such friendships, we don't just report on life events, but we tell where we believe God was in each event. We might ask a partner to help us break a task or purpose into bite-size pieces so we won't feel overwhelmed. We tell each other our dreams—what we would do if we could do anything, if time or money or obligations didn't inhibit us. We talk about the purpose that drives our dreams. For example, suppose you'd love to start a hideaway retreat center where women could escape when life gets to be too much, but that's not doable. Your friends can help you explore the purpose behind your dream—perhaps to provide safe emotional places for people. They can help you ask questions to determine if, for now, it would work to be known as a friend with an unlimited supply of teacups waiting for conversation or as a therapist volunteering at a "safe house" for battered women. You can dream together about what your purposes look like.

These sorts of partnership-friendships work only if we allow for differences. Judgment creates separation between friends, and many friendships have split up over Second Coming theology or whether it's best to send children to private school, public school, or to home school. For others, judgment arises because one wears polyester pants and imitation designer fragrances. People who think, act, and dress differently from us can add a great deal to our lives if we're open enough to come alongside them.

ACCOUNTABILITY

As trust grows, we get to the place where we can confess our faults to each other and be accountable: "Confess your sins to each other and pray for each other so that you may be healed. The prayer of a righteous man is powerful and effective" (James 5:16). Our hidden sin—jealousy of the person who gets more attention than we do, an attraction to the man who turns our head, the obnoxious thing said to the telemarketer on the phone yesterday—holds us back from purpose because we feel so unworthy. When we hide sin, it festers and grows until we become as sick as our secrets. The point is not that God doesn't use imperfect people, but that people who can admit their character flaws and negative attitudes surrender more easily to God.

Confessing to a friend brings healing because it makes my friend a witness to my relinquishment of compulsiveness, rage, and self-pity. I don't feel so driven to prove how wonderful I am. With her presence, there's more finality to my laying it all down.

On the listening side of transparent relationships, there can be no "fixing." Hearing a confession is a sign of honor, and we don't devalue it by dumping advice on that person, or Scripture verses or self-help books. We listen and pray. You might share an experience and ask, "Is that how it was for you?" but the purpose of sharing is not to give veiled advice, but to understand.

Partners hold each other accountable for procrastination, but we also laugh together at how easily distracted we become by things that have nothing to do with our purposes; laughter introduces grace. Then we plan to ask each other again. We commit to pray for each other and, if we both agree, report back on our progress.

The power of accountability comes from breaking my isolation and joining a team, not from fear that if I don't shape up, my friends will be disappointed in me. As I walk through the day and meet my problems, I have a strong sense that others are present with me. Because of their strength, I don't become entangled again. I could never stand in front of women and give retreats if I hadn't already set out my sins in front of people I trust.

If nothing else, accountability keeps us off a pedestal—which is where people may put us when we're involved in a purpose. Instead, we share our brokenness. I've watched purpose-filled women shed friends and even their spouse (emotionally, if not legally) because they are so driven. This is a mistake for so many reasons. Friends and family are the people who ground us. We seek their ideas not because they're experts (they may have nothing to do with our purposes), but because they know us and what is most likely to work for us.

An introvert by nature, I am continually tempted to fulfill my purposes for God as a "Lone Ranger," but that is a mistake. Intimate, accountable friendships help me serve others with humility and self-forgetfulness. Those qualities penetrate my character, and I come closer to my goal: to do the work of Christ with the heart of Christ.

QUESTIONS TO PONDER OR DISCUSS

1. Where do you find a sense of community?
2. Who has believed in you more than you have believed in yourself or has responded when you asked them to "stay here and keep watch"?
3. What magazines and books *could* shape your purpose in life?

EXPERIMENT IN LISTENING PRAYER

Ask God, *Who are the people you have brought to me to partner with?*

BIBLE PASSAGE TO CONTEMPLATE

> Therefore confess your sins to each other and pray for each other so that you may be healed. The prayer of a righteous man is powerful and effective. (James 5:16)

THIRTEEN

DREAMING
IN PURPOSEFUL WAYS

When I talk about purpose in life, some women respond by saying: "I know what breaks my heart, but I wouldn't know where to start." What they need is vision, and vision is fed by skills that flow not so much from the hands as from the mind and the heart.

A woman with purposes in her life is an entrepreneur of sorts. She's got to figure out how to make this dream happen—how to carve the time out of her demanding life, how to find resources in an economical way, and who will be the partners she'll ask to come alongside her. A foster parent, for example, has to spend time figuring out the age of children who would best fit in her family (babies? teens?) and where she'll start (align with a private or public agency?). With some framework to her dreams, she starts out—only to make thousands of revisions in the plans. Let's look at some of those intangible skills so important to a woman who wants to dream for God.

DEVELOPING YOUR DREAMING SKILLS

Every serious dreamer needs a notebook. In yours, you'll want to write about why your purpose is so necessary. Why is God involving you in this task instead of just doing it himself?

Then draw two columns: one for purposes and the other for tasks that carry out each purpose.

PURPOSES	TASKS
1) welcoming the strangers in this world	• opening my home to people who need somewhere to stay • keeping abreast of the refugee population in the world; teaching English as a second language to refugees here • talking to the people in my church about our church sponsoring refugees • greeting newcomers to my church and making sure they know how to find their children's classrooms

Once you have your list, reflect on it and ask God, *What stands in the way of doing what you are leading me to do?* Understand that dreaming may scare you. Don't feel bad if you hide the notebook and plan never to look at it again. Just keep asking God for further light and courage, and see what happens. In moments of courage, open the notebook to the "dreaming" tab and peek at it one more time.

After I've spent some time dreaming about tasks that would fulfill my purposes, I end that time by listing two or three actions I could attempt. Then I leave the idea alone without pressuring myself to do anything. I see what happens. Does God bring this idea or action items back to my mind? Am I scared? If so, why? Do I figure out that these ideas won't work? When that happens, I bounce my supposedly unworkable idea off a partner-friend or two. Often they will see what I don't—another ingredient needed, the tweak of the method. In time, these dreams and action items almost call out to me, *Yes, do this!* When this percolation process begins, everything looks too hard. But if I play with the ideas, I see how something might work out.

As I looked at my purpose of social justice, I knew I should pursue writing articles on that topic, but I felt overwhelmed. After much conviction, I sat down, shut my eyes, and poised my pen over a yellow legal-size pad of paper. *If I were really serious about this, I would…* After a few minutes I came up with ideas that required more time and money than I had. I stared at the pad of paper and asked God to show me how. I wrote "Action Item 1" and "Action Item 2." Then I left the space under these headings blank and put the pad away. In the next few days, I thought of several not-so-time-consuming baby steps for implementing these ideas. I wrote them down and put them in my notebook to revisit. The next thing I knew, I was writing them on my to-do list.

TRUST YOUR INSTINCTS

During this dreaming process, you'll have hunches. Don't be afraid to explore them. If you're infused with God, your hunches will be too. In Elizabeth Dole's speech at a Radcliffe commencement, she outlined several "female advantages" in public life. She urged these young female graduates to trust their instincts:

> It's not just female intuition—it's a cognitive skill that we are
> perhaps more open to. Estimation skills are now being taught
> to children as they come up through elementary and secondary
> schools, and instinct is oftentimes another word for it. It's an
> ability to take a great deal of information and quickly reduce it
> to a rough but generally accurate picture. It's the soft route to
> hard data.
>
> Yet, too often, we women allow ourselves to be intimidated
> into denying our instincts—whether it's a judgment of people,
> situations, or the heart of the policy question. The women in
> the audience have probably all had the experience of sitting
> across the table from someone with whom you disagree. Ask
> yourselves: How many times, in this situation, has your reac-
> tion been to question your own judgment rather than theirs—
> only to find out later that you were right on the money?
>
> Over the ages, we women have perfected to a high art form
> this trait of second-guessing ourselves. Perhaps it stems from
> our early constant exposure to society's message that female

traits and talents are inferior, but we have to get over it. It takes confidence to trust ourselves, and if we don't have confidence, our voices will be lost if ever they're heard.[1]

I find it difficult to trust my instincts, so my partners help me with this. I often ask my husband, "Here's what my instincts tell me; what do you think? Am I thinking clearly or is my attitude getting in the way?" Or I check with a friend, "I have this hunch; do you get the same impression?"

One of the benefits of dreaming is that it can help us set goals. Goal setting is about taking our dreams seriously and asking, "So what's the next step?" I shrink from asking that question because, if left to myself, I would sit in bed for the rest of my life curled up with a book and sipping a Diet Coke. A dream becomes a goal as I (1) figure out what steps to take to get there and (2) block out time in my calendar to take each of those steps. I keep these items in that same notebook, filed behind a tab labeled "goals."

Dreaming and goal setting—from a standpoint of spiritual development and knowing God—are not to help us achieve more and complete tasks more quickly. The purpose is to give us a focused heart: "I will give them singleness of heart and action, so that they will always fear me for their own good and the good of their children after them" (Jeremiah 32:39).

KEEPING THE DREAM ON COURSE

A purposeful woman will attract invitations to join this group or take on this task or head up committees. To keep from drifting from our purposes, we need to know when to say yes and no. At first, having purposes makes this easier because we focus on our purposes and let go of the rest. Then, too many opportunities come our way within our purposes, and we have to make mind-bending decisions. When I have to decide about allocating time to projects, I ask myself these questions:

- How well does this relate to one of my purposes in life?
- Who are my partners in this? Will I be working with people who have

a similar sense of mission in life? If I've dealt with these people before, what was that experience like?

- Is the event in which I'm asked to participate promoting God's purposes or promoting certain individuals?
- Is this a place where I can be salt and light to the world—perhaps where other Christians will not go?
- What unique experiences have prepared me for this?

Miriam Adeney says she sees fifteen sides to any situation and mulls endlessly on decisions. Here's how she decides to answer yes or no to projects and invitations:

- How important is it? How much power does it have to affect the world?
- How needy is it? Some things are important, but they don't require my attention. [The things that require *my* attention are usually *my* purposes.]
- Can or will anyone else do this, or am I uniquely fitted to do it by my gifts? Certain things will get done in your church whether or not you do them. I try to do the things that won't get done unless I do them.
- Is it new? Does it break ground? Will I grow? Or, is it something I have done before?
- Should I do this out of loyalty to family, friends, alma mater?
- What is the financial compensation? What are my needs at this time?
- Are my time and energy already committed elsewhere?[2]

CONSERVING ENERGY FOR DREAMING

To have the time and energy to dream, you'll need to organize and manage yourself by having systems—ways of doing things—in place. You can't always be fiddling with the details of life. You'll want to establish systems to take care of these things, so you can do them in your sleep. That way, you'll have a lot of creative energy left for the hard work of dreaming.

Systems, in the business sense, are specific procedures we use to do things: how we buy supplies; how we file business cards; how we organize addresses, books, even our wardrobe. Systems help us save time, but efficiency isn't the only goal. Systems help us spend our time in intentionally redemptive ways. Can you quickly locate the telephone number of the person you'd like to involve? Do you have a file system in place so you can find that statistic you know will motivate people to try harder? Are you organized enough to demonstrate you know where you're going, so the people who follow you can trust you and stay on board? Even if you're the only person you have to keep track of, you'll find your time is better used once you have systems in place to determine how you open your mail, which calendars you must keep current, where you save maps and directions, how often you retreat from this world to reflect and pray.

As a young pastor's wife at an urban church, I was deeply involved in youth work, so I began developing menus and shopping for groceries only once a month. I was—and am—by no means a superwife or housekeeper. I do it this way to give me more time and energy to do the things I believe God is calling me to do.

When you have systems in place—how you give to missions, where you go for retreat, who you rely on for decision making—you're not forever reinventing the wheel. I have included these in my notebook (under a tab labeled "procedure manual") because I'm liable to forget tomorrow the dandy systems I invent today. The best thing about this is that I no longer put off tasks I previously dreaded. They look much simpler now that they're written down. Systems free our minds of details, thus giving us clarity of mind and singleness of heart.

All these skills—dreaming, resiliency, decision making, system design—are not to be viewed as cogs in the self-improvement wheel. *Now I'm a better me!* They're simply tools that free us from anxiety and supply us with vision and energy, so we can stay focused and continue to enjoy our journey with God.

QUESTIONS TO PONDER AND DISCUSS

1. Look at your track record as a mistake maker. How did your parents respond when things were going well? Think of an accomplishment you are proud of; what mistakes did you make in the process?
2. What would you do in life if you knew you would not fail? Consider this for a few minutes.
3. Consider the two lists of questions to guide decision making presented in this chapter. Which questions would be yours? What would you add?

EXPERIMENT IN LISTENING PRAYER

Ask God, *What skills of dreaming, resiliency, or decision making have I avoided in the past? Give me courage to pursue them.*

BIBLE PASSAGE TO CONTEMPLATE

> I will give them *singleness of heart* and action, so that they will always fear me for their own good and the good of their children after them. (Jeremiah 32:39, emphasis added)

FOURTEEN

BRING YOUR BROKENNESS TO GOD

K aren* puts her head in her hands and sobs. She feels like she's two people—one she likes, one she hates. Karen volunteers in an enrichment program for hearing-impaired children. She is compassionate and patient with the children, but she can't stand the other adult volunteers. They aren't quick enough with their sign language, and they don't try as hard as she does.

The supervisor of the program would love to make Karen her assistant, but Karen's sharpness with the other volunteers prevents it. After she blasted them one day, she went home and tried to nap and forget it, but her family was too noisy. Since she couldn't nap, she pouted for the rest of the evening.

Karen is purposeful about ministering to the hearing-impaired, but she is also driven by "the committee in her head"—voices telling her to measure up, do better, prove herself. She was the youngest in her family, deemed incapable of anything significant, so she strives to do better, work harder, be more in this life.

Many women have found their purposes aborted because of their inner neediness. Many of us have passion, but we also have envy, divisiveness, and selfish ambition (Galatians 5:19-20). Our moodiness prevents us from getting

*not her real name

along with others in God's "family business." But our brokenness can be healed as we work out our purposes.

In order for God to have freedom to work his purposes in us, we need to offer him our destructive attitudes and motives. If I invite a woman who's struggling financially to live in my empty guest room, I won't be of help to her unless my inner neediness has been addressed. If we are needy, we will pursue our purposes with a self-serving agenda, expressed by a committee of voices in our head:

- the voice of despair *(I'll never make it.)*
- the voice of fear *(Get out of this uncomfortable situation!)*
- the voice that creates conflict *(Set this person straight!)*
- the voice of self-doubt *(I'm so dumb—I'll never get this.)*
- the voice of ambition *(I must be successful, fulfilled, and well-dressed so people will value me.)*
- the voice of self-protection *(This looks scary. I'll quit now so no one can say I failed.)*
- the voice of self-justification *(It's her fault I didn't succeed.)*

Giving in to these voices results in sins such as self-promotion, willfulness, and self-abasement, each of which grow from a core of brokenness. We all desire to be loved and valued. When those needs aren't met, our brokenness snowballs and we become needy for affirmation and reinforcement. As we do so, we find it difficult to cooperate with others. Instead, we distance ourselves from them, suffocate them with attention, or offend them with our impatience for love and value.

PROVING MYSELF TO MYSELF

Success is sometimes more a sign of being driven than of God's hand at work. The wealthy Nabal was successful, but his servants turned to his wife, Abigail, for a creative, peaceful solution because they knew their master lacked character (1 Samuel 25). In her book *New Passages,* Gail Sheehy describes a successful fashion designer, Jill, who wanted to switch careers to prove herself once more. In her mind, life is about "accomplishing dreams and being impossibly young always." Jill had her own "gratification fantasy": "Once I become rich and powerful, no one can ever make me feel small or second-class again or treat me like a helpless little boy or girl."[1]

We don't have to be a glamorous success to crave love and admiration. When my husband was a young pastor, I needed to prove I was capable, so I did every possible job a pastor's wife could do and became president of every group. When I confess this as I lead retreats, many heads nod in understanding. We have performed not because we can do all things through Christ who strengthens us, but because we're going to prove to the world we know which end is up and we can fix it all by next Tuesday, thank you. After years of God's reshaping and refining, it still shocks me that I can serve on a committee without thinking I could do a better job of leading it.

As typical religious people, we tend to prove our worth through workaholism, or what I call being "hooked on productivity." This is when I say yes to whatever is asked of me, particularly if it makes me look good. My addiction to productivity tells me to make sure I do the best job that's ever been done. I hike down a "career path" faster and farther than anyone else my age. I hurry life away, discovering just how much cleaning and filing I can get done while talking on the telephone. I confess I still get an adrenaline high when I can cross off everything on my daily to-do list.

How do we know when we're hooked on productivity? When work is more important than going to the doctor or dentist; when we feel frantic about getting things done; when tears come for no reason. If we're driven in unhealthy ways, we don't rest when we're tired, we can't cry when we're hurt, we don't ask for help when we need it. We think it's our purpose that's driving us, but it's really our inner neediness.

Neediness forces us to do whatever will gain people's approval instead of following what we've already discerned as breaking our heart and the heart of God. We make decisions by second-guessing other people's thoughts instead of engaging in the back-and-forth conversation with God that he desires and we desperately need.

People pleasing is subtle. It's difficult to discern legitimate sensitivity to people's needs from sensitivity to their like or dislike of us. If we work with teens, for example, it's easy to care more about whether they like us than whether we're genuinely helping them. Following our purpose requires an ability to stand alone, to be different, to make choices that confuse other people...all of which is impossible to do if we are looking for approval.

DOING THE WORK OF CHRIST WITH THE HEART OF CHRIST

To follow through with our purposes, we need to face the voices of our brokenness and choose to live an examined life. Then we not only find redemption in Christ, but we also behave redemptively in this world. We can fulfill God's will, which is that Christ be formed in us and our character be transformed: "the glorious riches of this mystery, which is Christ in you, the hope of glory" (Colossians 1:27). God is more interested in who we are than in what we can do for him, whether we're starting a counseling center or scrubbing floors for a chronically ill person. God transforms us inwardly, so *we* are the work: "For it is God who works in you to will and to act according to his good purpose" (Philippians 2:13).

As God works in us, we shed our inner neediness and talk back to the committee in our head by admitting we have large, gaping sores: fear, inadequacy, grandiosity.

WHEN THE INNER CRITIC SAYS...	WE ANSWER...
• Be better.	• God is in charge of the transformation process.
• You'll never make it.	• True, but God will move forward and I plan to ride on his coattails.
• Maybe you're to blame for this entire mess.	• Maybe, maybe not. Either way, I'm going to help fix the problem instead of fixing blame. How can I help?

Because I've seen how neediness can get in the way, I've learned with every step of service to ask, *Is this about me, or is this about you, God? Is what I sniff the burning desire God put within me or my own ego aflame? Was that great idea I had the voice of God or the voice of my ego wanting to look important?* I know it's about me if, when the job is done, I care more about what kind of impression I left rather than whether God's love was shown and the kingdom of God was advanced.

We must recognize voices of self-absorption and surrender them in order to have clarity about our true passions. Basil Pennington tells about asking Mother Teresa of Calcutta for a word of life for the brothers at his monastery. Finally, she said, slowly and with great emphasis, "Tell them to pray that I do not get in God's way."[2] This Trappist monk comments:

> Most of our lives bear so little fruit because we are ever getting into God's way with our own plans, our own doings, our own fears. The false self is a construct we create out of what we have, what we do, what others think of us. We in our falseness do get in God's way. The God who is truth does not work through the false self. When we sit in the silence, doing nothing, having nothing, letting go of all our own thoughts and imaginings, all our memories and feelings, we die to the false self. And in the clearing we come to know God, and that without God we can do *nothing*.[3]

When we get in God's way, it's easy to think, *I've found my purpose in life. What I'm doing is important.* We forget that the motives in our hearts as we serve are as important as the service itself—perhaps more so.

Here are some questions I ask myself regularly to reveal how I need God to teach me to do the work of Christ with the heart of Christ.

Am I serving to impress anyone? It's difficult to say no to tasks that bring recognition, perhaps not to ourselves, but to our children or spouse or the company for which we work. We don't admit it even to ourselves, but there aren't many of us who have prayed aloud in a group and not felt disappointed because someone "took" what we were going to say. Were we praying to God or to impress others? Few people volunteer to do something considered unsuccessful. I observed this when a children's program was being phased out and no one wanted to help the last month. The same kids were involved in that program as in the newer, glitzy one, but serving children with the heart of Christ was not the central issue. What mattered was being connected to the newer, supposedly successful program.

Am I serving to receive external rewards? While we're often embarrassed by obvious, external rewards, we do tend to want some form of recognition. When I was leading a support group, I felt slighted because someone in the church referred to our group as the "losers." Then we were inadvertently left out of the directory's list of ministries. So one night when I arrived, I thought about leaving a note for the pastor. I figured I could write a note about something—anything would do—but it would begin with, "While I was here for the support group Wednesday night...." Then he'd remember how important our group was and how faithfully I showed up to lead the group. But then my partner walked up, and I began thinking about how she and I had gotten involved in this because we had a heart for hurting people. At that point, I discarded my plan. I remember saying to God, *I got in this for you, but I've gotten sidetracked.* Since then, I've asked myself, *Would I still do this if no one ever found out?* I would like to have motives so pure that rewards wouldn't matter.

Is my service affected by moods and whims? I've noticed that the call to do something seems much stronger when the other participants are fun and pleasant. If they're grouchy, I'm definitely not called to serve on that committee!

Am I using this service to feel good about myself? At a banquet once I heard someone complain that the lettuce was cut, not torn. Why hadn't they taken the time to do it *right?* I made a mental note that whenever I was in charge, the lettuce would be torn, not cut. I found I had an insatiable need to top whatever happened at last year's banquet.

The real issue was that I wanted to be a star instead of a servant. Whenever we suspect this might be the case, it's time to get alone with God. Times of solitude allow us to hear the voice of God showing us our true motives and inviting us to change. Says Richard Foster, "It is an occupational hazard of devout people to confuse their work with God's work. How easy it is to replace 'this work is really significant' with 'I am really significant.'"[4]

Am I using my service to muffle God's voice demanding I change? Have you ever been a part of a ministry or program in which the people in charge needed to grow up? Maybe they loved the limelight or lost their temper a lot. If the program was a success, those people probably didn't change. That's because, as Eugenia Price, writes, "It is far easier to serve than to be changed."[5]

As long as we're successful, we probably won't listen to God's voice demanding that we change unless we work at hearing it. As people thank us and admire our skill, we forget how we've hurt or ignored others, and God's voice is stifled.

HEALING IS NOT A PREREQUISITE

None of this is to say, however, that we cannot serve until our brokenness is healed. Character development isn't the first step in pursuing a purpose-full life because "character develops by attaching yourself to and being true to a story that is bigger than yourself."[6] Besides, it isn't until we get into the trenches of service that our character flaws emerge so clearly. The danger is that we become so busy *doing* that we forget to look at *being* and *character*. Ideally, service and inner growth progress alongside each other, and we never stop growing. The more we seek God and his purposes, the more likely we are to develop a pure heart and feel secure in God. "When you are doing something that deeply expresses who you are and you feel this is the will of God, you don't need to have so much fame and popularity," says Miriam Adeney. "When you're doing what you're created to do, it's so satisfying you don't need external affirmation. You need friends, but not fame."

LINKING UP WITH THE ONE WHO LOVES US

The struggle to believe we have great worth to God is universal. Even women who have great jobs, are happily married, have stellar children, and are drop-dead gorgeous talk as if God is out to get them instead of out to save them.

In reality you are the one for whom the shepherd left the ninety-nine sheep (Luke 15:1-7). The shepherd risked the lives of those other sheep, leaving them defenseless, to find you because you might be lost or stuck in a crevice or just too discouraged to figure out how to get home. Some commentators suggest that a shepherd in those times would never have abandoned the ninety-nine sheep in the open country, and so Jesus must have meant that the shepherd left them in a sheepfold or with another shepherd. Jesus' radical story, however, doesn't say that. No sheepfold or substitute shepherd is mentioned. What kind of shepherd was the star of Jesus' story? A rash redeemer who cares passionately about you, the lost, wandering sheep wishing she knew her way back. Perhaps Jesus intended for the radical behavior of the shepherd to underscore the theme that God pursues each of us no matter what—especially since he told the parable in response to the huffy Pharisees muttering over his fraternizing with "sinners."[7] Jesus wanted us to know that God loves each of us in the same reckless, passionate way.

Sadly, our love relationship with God is often poisoned by notions that God is not a caring shepherd but a bad-tempered overseer, and so we put harsh words in his mouth. It's as if we paraphrase Matthew 11:29 to say, "Take my yoke upon you and groan from me, for I am grouchy and harsh of heart, and you will find exhaustion for your souls," instead of "Take my yoke upon you and learn from me, for I am gentle and humble in heart, and you will find rest for your souls."

I thought about this as I interviewed Christine Aroney-Sine, who you may remember was forced home by chronic fatigue syndrome. When I asked if all her hard work had contributed to it, she replied, "There's some truth in that. When I look back, I can see signals I was overworking myself when there were alternatives. I didn't know how to say no. The people around me didn't know how to say no. I felt the pressure to keep going." Christine points to the love relationship with God as the central issue: "I and those around me hadn't learned lessons of listening to God that would have relieved the pressure. God isn't a hard taskmaster, wanting us to burn out or overwork ourselves. People who have that view of God never hear God telling them to say no to anything. Christian activity is not doing things for God, but being rooted in God."

It's my responsibility to live and breathe the truth that I am desperately loved even if I never become famous, look good for my age, own a new home, or make significant amounts of money. I have often meditated on the parable of the lost sheep and found that, as I'm carried home on the shoulders of the shepherd, I can feel great satisfaction even when no one else notices me. I feel loved in this world by God even when no one affirms me. Even though the work sitting on my desk is flawed, I can feel adequate because I am loved by the Father who made the tree outside my window.

Those inner voices of fear, inadequacy, and grandiosity must be answered for the rest of our lives with God's simple message, "How great is the love the Father has lavished on us, that we should be called children of God!" (1 John 3:1). No doubt it will take the rest of our lives to believe this truth in such a way that our behavior is affected and our service is untainted by self-promotion.

When we grasp the truth that God loves us, our inner wounds begin to heal. His love empowers us to be molded by him. As we feel more secure in God's true identity as the daring, caring shepherd, we can trust God enough to ask him the tough question: "How are you trying to change me?" It doesn't hurt so much to hear painful things, because we rest secure in the sense of being loved. Wrote Evelyn Underhill, author and translator, "We can never become un-selfed on our own—it is God's work in us. We can only open the door and say, 'Do what You like.'"[8]

QUESTIONS TO PONDER OR DISCUSS
1. Which voices most often lead to failure of character in your life?
   - the voice of despair
   - the voice of fear
   - the voice that creates conflict
   - the voice of self-doubt
   - the voice of ambition
   - the voice of self-protection
   - the voice of self-justification
2. Which of the questions listed in this chapter under "Doing the Work of Christ with the Heart of Christ" are most convicting to you?

EXPERIMENT IN LISTENING PRAYER
Ask God, *What activities do I do to be loved or admired?*

BIBLE PASSAGE TO CONTEMPLATE
As you read these verses, picture yourself as the sheep being carried home after the shepherd has searched diligently for you.

> Suppose one of you has a hundred sheep and loses one of them. Does he not leave the ninety-nine in the open country and go after the lost sheep until he finds it? And when he finds it, he joyfully puts it on his shoulders and goes home. Then he calls his friends and neighbors together and says, "Rejoice with me; I have found my lost sheep." I tell you that in the same way there will be more rejoicing in heaven over one sinner who repents than over ninety-nine righteous persons who do not need to repent. (Luke 15:4-7)

SECTION FOUR

STAYING ON TRACK

FIFTEEN

WHEN YOU FEEL
LIKE QUITTING

O ne danger I've learned to avoid is the temptation to romanticize the idea of standing before a burning bush, sensing a call, and then following it. Even when we follow God's purposes for our lives, we get tired physically and emotionally. We deal with people we would rather avoid. We may feel as if we don't have a clue to what's going on.

As I interviewed women of purpose for this book, one of the common threads I heard was perseverance. And why not? This rugged, hard-edged character trait is rooted in continual surrender to God. Perseverance equips us to go on when other volunteers quit, when the sponsoring organization goes out of business, or when our visionary leader runs out of inspiration. Perseverance keeps us in the chair working when we'd rather do anything—even wash dishes—than tackle the task in front of us.

Oswald Chambers offered this picture of perseverance:

> A saint's life is in the hands of God like a bow and arrow in the hands of an archer. God is aiming at something the saint cannot see, but our Lord continues to stretch and strain, and every once in a while the saint says, "I can't take anymore." Yet God pays no attention; He goes on stretching until His purpose is in sight, and then He lets the arrow fly."[1]

This portrait of perseverance describes our partnership with God. Even when we've agreed to do challenging tasks that make us uncomfortable, we get up in the morning to partner with God. If the project fails or is rejected, God's living, breathing presence remains a constant. We agonize over being stretched and pulled, but we trust God enough that when the arrow flies, we're grateful.

POINT OF NO RETURN

Earlier in this book you met Elsie Purnell—missionary, stateside mission representative, and missionary kids' advocate whose purpose is to do God's will by communicating the gospel, especially to the people of northern Thailand. Elsie says perseverance looks like persistent obedience. "Our friends and relatives in New Jersey asked us, 'Why would you live in California? Your house burned down [in the Altadena fires], your daughter was murdered.' I live in California for the same reason I lived in Thailand for thirteen years. I'm here because this is where God led us to advance the work in Thailand from this side of the ocean.

"Sometimes it's difficult here, but life was difficult living in a tribal village in Thailand. I had three children under three and a half in diapers. Everything I cooked was from scratch. We had a dirt floor and no privacy—the bamboo in the walls of the outhouse and bedroom spread apart and 'grew eyes.' I didn't live there because I liked it. I lived there because God called me to care about the Mien people of northern Thailand."

What motivated Elsie to continue? "I never could have endured the first term without a firm call." She had been attending prayer meetings for Southeast Asia as a student at Moody Bible Institute when one night, "the attendance was terrible and the leader droned on," says Elsie. "But with everything that came out of his mouth, it was as if God said, *This is what I want you to do.* It confirmed my call and my link with Overseas Missionary Fellowship."

But what about her boyfriend, Herb, from back East? "He came to visit me at Moody Bible Institute, but he thought God didn't want him to marry me and so it was over. We went to a prayer meeting together, but the room was so crowded we couldn't sit together. When I saw the film about northern Thailand, I thought, *God, whether or not Herb goes, I will go.* During the film, Herb was touched too. On the el that night, he talked about going to Thailand, but he needed a 'secretary.' That was how God pulled us together."

During the tough times, Elsie relied on these defining moments. In these moments we choose once and for all to be who God is calling us to be.

Defining moments often occur during crisis. We have to make a decision, and that decision defines our mission. Amid grief and desperation, the Moabite woman Ruth faced the defining moment of her life in her radical decision to go with her mother-in-law to become a part of God's nation, Israel: "Don't urge me to leave you or to turn back from you. Where you go I will go, and where you stay I will stay. Your people will be my people and your God my God. Where you die I will die, and there I will be buried. May the LORD deal with me, be it ever so severely, if anything but death separates you and me" (Ruth 1:16-17).

When Naomi tried to persuade her daughter-in-law not to take this step, Ruth would have none of it. Try to imagine that first day Ruth went out to participate in Israel's welfare system, gleaning leftover grain in the fields. Perhaps she sang like Snow White with birds fluttering around her—but probably not. We do know that she rolled up her sleeves and gathered grain. (Defining moments help us persevere when our purposes call for tedious or humiliating tasks.) Based on the outcome—a Gentile woman holding a permanent place in the Jewish heritage of Christ (Matthew 1:5)—this woman obviously heard the voice of God within her, pulling her to her heart's purpose.

Our defining moments may occur when someone makes fun of our purpose or the tasks attached to it. I mentioned earlier that someone important to me once minimized my curriculum writing—"so you're writing those little teacher's books"—and I ended up explaining passionately my desire for people to know God in an authentic way. That was a defining moment for me. I'd staked out my territory and stated my calling to a hostile recipient. And I didn't care how silly I may have appeared to that person.

Defining moments feed our perseverance because they become "moments of no return." In the face of great odds, we understand once and for all what we're called to do. As a young missionary in the rural south, JoeAnn Ballard (foster parent and Neighborhood Christian Center founder) built a Sunday school from absolutely nothing, but a few years later she found her spirit paralyzed. "What stopped me in my tracks were the sting of births, miscarriages, and tubal pregnancies," she says. "I was a silent person who didn't share my feelings. I felt such pain (both physically and emotionally) and couldn't get anyone to understand how I hurt.

"It was Christmas and I was eight months pregnant. After a party with 250 kids in my house, I felt I had spent all I could spend of me. I'd reached out to other kids as much as I could. I said to my husband, 'Enough is enough. I can't do this.' Monroe said, 'If you stop now, you'll be sorry. You'll look back and say you quit when you needed to go ahead.' It was what I needed to hear. Through the months, I improved. This dark time forced me to talk about feelings and work through my struggle with inadequacy."

JoeAnn says that this was the lowest point in her life, but "God showed me he was God. He settled my life over those years. Now, no matter how dark the situation is, I've already been there and I know he can deliver it." These defining moments become a tower we can point back to and remember, much like the twelve-stone memorial the Israelites built to remind themselves of God's miraculous faithfulness after crossing the Jordan River (Joshua 4:1-9). These memorable experiences give us something to point to and say, "This is when I knew God wanted me to...."

LEARNING FROM FAILURE

Defining moments often come when we fail, which we do over and over. The goal, however, is not to stop failing, but to become a resilient person. Many of the biblical figures we admire were blunderers, but they surrendered to God and bounced back. Peter denied Jesus three times and felt enormous guilt, but he responded to Jesus' presence on the shore and was reconciled to him (John 21:4-17). When you fail, imagine God responding as Jesus did to Peter's failure. Jesus didn't ignore Peter, but singled him out for conversation. Jesus didn't seem to be mad at Peter, but helped him look at his inner motives. Jesus accepted Peter's less-than-perfect answers and gave Peter a commission—feed the sheep—even though he had failed once already. Jesus kept challenging Peter to love him and to do his work on earth.[2] Do you see God responding this way to your failures?

Rather than being discouraged by our failures, we can commit ourselves to learn from them. Failure can become our "counsel" and "many advisers": "Plans fail for lack of counsel, but with many advisers they succeed" (Proverbs 15:22). Or as my friend's ballet teacher said, "Mistakes are data. Use them."

Robert Mauer, Ph.D., director of behavioral science at Santa Monica UCLA Medical Center, has studied the art and science of making mistakes. He says people have two inaccurate ideas about mistakes: "One is believing that other people have it easier and don't make mistakes. They don't have it easier, although we believe they do. The other is that we think the more successful we are, the fewer mistakes we make." In fact, Mauer says, the more creative, diligent, and hard working people are, the more mistakes they make.[3]

Dolores Feitl has found one of her purposes in life to be ministry to pastors' spouses. As a result, she founded POWER (Pastors' Outreaching Wives Enrichment Resource), an advocacy group for pastors' wives. Part of her role involves planning events such as luncheons and retreats, something at which she is clearly skilled. Eighteen years ago when she was in charge of a women's ministries program, her first event was going to be the "best luncheon that ever happened!" says Dolores. "I worked and worked to make this the event of the year, anticipating at least sixty women. Things weren't usually done with this much flair, but I felt strongly that it be this way. When only ten women showed up, I felt like a public failure."

Dolores complained to her Bible study leader, who kept asking her, "Why did you plan this event?" Dolores gave the standard answers: She loved God and she cared about women. The wise leader asked, "Did the women feel cared for?" "Well, yes," Dolores answered. "Then in reality you succeeded. Why do you think you're so unhappy? Are you sure that was your goal?" the leader probed.

Dolores was angry but said nothing. Finally, as she came before God she was able to understand and admit that she planned the event to look successful and to help her husband—an up-and-coming executive—appear like a winner. But the wives of her husband's peers hadn't shown up. Today, she plans all kinds of events, keeping in mind the wisdom acquired from her "mistake" and public failure: Serve with a whole heart whomever comes.

We examine our mistakes not to punish ourselves but to evaluate why we made them. "Failure can be one of the most useful experiences of adult life, but only for those who stop long enough to learn from it," wrote Gail Sheehy in *New Passages.* She went on to describe a woman who repeatedly finds it too threatening to evaluate her failures. "She cuts her losses, cauterizes her emotions, and springs forward double time to find the next hurdle."[4] Is that you?

OUR PARTNERS CAN KEEP US GOING

Another building block of perseverance is the encouragement we receive from our "partners"—our friends, relatives, and especially role models. Miriam Adeney talks about having her first baby on December 1, the day she also needed to grade her college students' semester term papers. "I came home from the hospital and figured I would turn the term papers in late. Because my mother is family-oriented, I thought she'd concur, but she handed me the term papers and said, 'You have a job. Do it. Don't wimp out.' I learned from her example. As a professional person I've learned that if you want to be taken seriously in life and be given responsibilities, you have to fulfill them with excellence." Our partners help us keep on when we feel like quitting.

Our partners also can help us learn from failure. It's easy to be too proud to tell a friend about our failures, but they can provide us with the encouragement we need—they've been walking alongside us for a while and can help us evaluate the situation. As Henrietta Mears trained teachers, assistants, and college students, she "saw to it that a leader was not allowed to remain in failure." On occasion, college evangelistic teams would come back almost in tears. "She would sit them down and say, 'All right now, why did you fail?' Then the reasons came to light: The program had not been thought through far enough in advance, Bob had not been prepared to preach, Louis hadn't figured out… As all this was discussed, a metamorphosis took place. Now the causes for failure were understood, and with ways for overcoming them in view, the team could hardly be kept from racing out and holding another meeting."[5]

Sometimes when I've failed, I've put myself in the above scene. I see a wise woman full of grace going over the details with me. Was it this? Or this? So I browse through a familiar book on the subject and ask God to show me what I missed. Sometimes just the thought of the graceful presence of God, always accepting me no matter what, is enough.

DEVELOPING EYES OF FAITH

On an ordinary, day-to-day level, perseverance requires the ability to see beyond the moment, which demands an optimism that is not a pie-in-the-sky oblivion or even positive thinking. Rather, this optimism is characterized by redemptive thinking and facing reality while believing God is in charge. Let's look at some characteristics of earthy, faith-based optimism.

Expect problems. When we understand and accept that life is full of opposition, we don't perch atop the naive end of the teetertotter and slide down when trouble strikes. Peter warned the early Christians, "Dear friends, do not be *surprised* at the painful trial you are suffering, as though something strange were happening to you" (1 Peter 4:12, emphasis added). Surprise intensifies our pain. We're caught off guard by flawed leaders, canceled contracts, and dwindling commitment. Our naiveté becomes putty in Satan's hands as our high expectations undo us. In contrast, when we expect problems, we're prepared to deal with them and we readily turn to God for solutions.

Adopt a spirit of determination. From a dirty prison cell, Paul repeatedly declared, "I press on…" (Philippians 3:12,14). Paul didn't lose sight of the big picture of spreading God's word. He understood that in God's plan he was a missionary even when he was in jail. His purpose didn't end when his circumstances changed. He simply switched audiences—from Gentile crowds to prison guards.

Feed on positive thoughts. Paul's prison ministry also flourished because he concentrated on the things in life that tasted of God: Whatever was true, noble, right, pure, lovely, and admirable (Philippians 4:8). Paul wasn't proposing an unrealistic, "smiles only" approach. A few verses earlier he mentioned problems caused by a dispute between two Philippian women (Philippians 4:2). He acknowledged problems and suggested solutions, but he advised his readers not to dwell on those things.

One tool that helps me maintain a bigger perspective is what one of my college professors called a "footwarmer" file. It includes thank-you cards and notes of encouragement that celebrate how God has worked through an ordinary person like me. They warm the spirit just as thick socks warm feet on a cold night. One of my earliest "footwarmers" was the impressive business card of a young Latino man I taught in Sunday school when I was first trying to help students participate more in the learning process. At that time, he was a shy, disinterested junior-high-school student on the fringes of gang activity. When I found out he could draw, I began using art activities I had been uncomfortable with. After that, he trusted me. All those encouraging words, pats on the back, and sluggish conversations eventually paid off. As I began writing curriculum, I kept his card in front of me.

Stay open to unknown factors. We think we know exactly what will happen, but we don't. We may feel that a partner has ignored us or we need to change jobs, only to find out the friend was preoccupied with a stomachache and we're being promoted at work. We can't anticipate everything, but we can learn to expect surprises and strive to be flexible. "In his heart a man plans his course, but the LORD determines his steps" (Proverbs 16:9). God always has the last word.

WHEN TASKS WITHIN YOUR PURPOSE CHANGE

How can we keep focusing on our purpose if our tasks change or end? Let's say you work at a college helping young adults with spiritual formation. A

budget cut is needed, and your position is terminated. How will you participate in the spiritual formation of others now? Or let's say you're a nurturer
and nest-builder, but your kids grow up, leave home, and go off to become
adults. Whom will you nurture? What nests will you build?

Circumstances frequently change, but purposes remain the same. Your
job or vocation may change, but your heart remains unchanged and you long
to fulfill your purposes.

After working twelve years as a doctor on the *Anastasis,* Christine Aroney-
Sine now lives in the United States and fulfills her purpose of being an advocate for the poor through speaking, writing, and training. I asked her how she
continued to stay focused on Third-World issues (in other words, stay "in
flow") when her life is now so insulated from worldwide poverty. She mentioned five things that help focus her efforts—and that can help us as well.

1. Scripture. "I read the gospels regularly and continually ask myself, How
did Christ live and how would he live in our present age? I work with great
intentionality for transformation in my life to make God's purposes my purposes: sight for the blind, release for the prisoners, and good news to the poor."

2. Reading material. "I seek out and make sure I read on a regular basis
books that challenge me with the way I believe God would have us live—'living more simply so others may simply live.' I read magazines that keep me up
to speed on global issues."

3. Partners. "Tom [her husband] and I stay connected with groups that
work in overseas missions, and we try to spend as much time as possible
with people who are constantly immersed in these needs."

4. Experience. "We would like to take a trip to a Third-World country
each year, but my health has not allowed that. At this point my best 'focusing' practice is to spend time with people who are living and working in the
Third World with the poorest of the poor."

5. Reflection and prayer. "We take a few days every few months for a
prayer retreat. This is a time to focus on our relationship with God and to
make sure that the things we think should be priorities in our lives really are
occupying most of our time and energy."

When we stay focused in these ways, God can continue to shape us and our purposes, and we won't be distracted by forty-five other wonderful things to do. We can trust that God really is in charge, and he is showing us what to do today and what comes next tomorrow. We can persevere.

QUESTIONS TO PONDER OR DISCUSS

1. What would help you stay focused on the task? footwarmers? partners? on-site experiences?

2. When, if ever, have you experienced a defining moment in which you chose a purpose or course of action within it and knew you'd never turn back?

EXPERIMENT IN LISTENING PRAYER

Ask God, *Are my purposes and priorities occupying most of my time and energy?*

BIBLE PASSAGE TO CONTEMPLATE

Ponder Colossians 3:16, phrase by phrase:

- Let the word of Christ dwell in you richly
- as you teach and admonish one another with all wisdom, and
- as you sing psalms, hymns and spiritual songs
- with gratitude in your hearts to God.

SIXTEEN

MOVING AROUND
THE OBSTACLES

If I'd been a friend or fellow synagogue member of Esther of the Old Testament, I would have been appalled that this nice Jewish girl would enter a beauty contest in order to marry a pagan! Why wasn't she focusing on "inner beauty" instead of spending a year primping for a beauty pageant? Even if she was forced to participate in the contest, as some commentators speculate, I might have said, "Sure, but she doesn't have to enjoy it so much!" Then when she won, I would have crossed her off my list altogether ("Look at the people she hangs out with!"), predicting that she would forget God after she mixed with Persian royalty and political power plays. Or, even worse, I might have exploited her as my new, useful contact in the palace. I can hardly imagine myself commending Esther for pursuing her purpose in life.

You and I can depend on a similar response from some of the people in our lives. If you are a forward-moving person, you may not be popular, especially if you're trying to pull an already existing program or organization closer to God's purposes. People are maintenance-oriented and want life to remain the same. Jesus, for example, was forward moving, pointing toward a fresh vision of the kingdom of God and how God *so loves the world,* while the Pharisees were interested in maintaining Jewish tradition with strict Sabbath-keeping and hand-washing laws. This is one more part of expecting problems instead of being surprised by them (1 Peter 4:12).

WISDOM TO FACE CRITICISM

From the maintenance-oriented person's viewpoint, the forward-moving person is messing things up. If the women's group has craft nights and you suggest they write letters to prisoners or visit women in a home for unwed mothers, expect resistance. (It's often easier to start something new and add it to the schedule than to change an existing item.) On the other hand, we're good at being victims, and so we confuse God's work with our whims. Although criticism may be painful, you're not being persecuted when people don't like the theme you picked for the annual spring fling or when they don't volunteer for your pet project.

Purity of motives is essential when responding to criticism: "Above all else, guard your heart, for it is the wellspring of life. Put away perversity from your mouth; keep corrupt talk far from your lips. Let your eyes look straight ahead, fix your gaze directly before you" (Proverbs 4:23-25). In this way, purpose in life is so much about *being*. As you're doing these tasks to which God called you, you let God shape your inner person into "Christ in you, the hope of glory" (Colossians 1:27).

But how do we find this saintlike courage to resist returning evil for evil and insult for insult? It helps if we bring that criticism immediately to God. We have permission to rail as the writers of the imprecatory psalms did. (Although, they often mellowed their rantings toward the end by thanking God for past deliverances, and it would serve us well to do the same. Psalm 3 is a good example.) This railing is an excellent way to surrender the person and circumstance to God, and it can keep us from using that inner heat to return insults.

When someone uses you as a target for gossip and criticism over a long period of time, what can you do? If we're working for God's purposes of reconciliation, we have to live like reconcilers. If we're interested in redeeming a group of people—say, juvenile felons—then we'll also be interested in redeeming our critics. So we stay away from judgment and condemnation; we don't return insults; we refuse to gossip; we don't withdraw. We wait for an opportunity for reconciliation: "Therefore, if you are offering your gift at the altar and there remember that your brother has something against you, leave your gift there in front of the altar. First go and be reconciled to your brother; then come and offer your gift" (Matthew 5:23-24). Somehow we let go of the need to defend ourselves, and if we are able, we say, "I'm willing to listen to whatever you have to say." The goal is to see the person's heart. I sometimes close my eyes and ask God, *What does this person need? Are you calling me to meet any of those needs?*

We can expect to be criticized even by the people we serve. Christine Aroney-Sine tells about when the *Anastasis* staff worked in a hospital in Mexico:

> It wasn't easy to adapt from the efficiency and task-oriented nature of a Western hospital to a more relaxed relationship-based situation. Every day, some new obstacle stopped us from achieving our goals. Once, there was no power at the hospital and we waited impatiently for its reconnection. Sometimes the water was turned off, or the autoclave didn't work and we had no instruments. At times the patients were late, or an emergency operation delayed us. We became angry and frustrated by the slow pace.
>
> "Why don't you take time to talk to us?" the hospital staff asked one day as we impatiently paced back and forth in the empty recovery room. "You're always too busy," they admonished us, their brown faces puckering with concern. They wanted to ask about our families, our lives, and our faith. All we seemed interested in was our work and how to make our procedures more efficient.
>
> Their complaint was justified. In our Western society, getting the job done tends to be far more important than making friends and developing relationships. We love numbers and statistics and tend to judge our efforts in quantities not qualities. We need to slow down and learn to listen to the people around us.[1]

Upon self-examination, Christine saw that her coworkers' criticism had merit. This is usually the case, but occasionally the reproach is unwarranted and we're stumped at how to respond. Here are some guidelines I gleaned from Jesus' story of the way a father handled disagreements with two types of people: his prodigal son and his dutiful son (Luke 15:11-32).

HOW TO COPE WITH WRONGDOER CRITICS (THE YOUNGER SON)	HOW TO COPE WITH SELF-IMPORTANT KNOW-IT-ALL CRITICS (THE OLDER SON)
• Don't try to control them—let them go. • Don't expect them to behave in an exemplary way. • Expect to watch them go through a lot of pain. • Keep looking for a change of heart. • Welcome and affirm a change of heart without recounting their past wrong deeds.	• Expect them to be jealous of the graciousness you show to others. • Don't expect them to be above withdrawing or lashing out at you in anger. • Let them express that anger. • Reassure them of their value to you and others. • Remind them to rejoice when God's purposes are accomplished.

The "wrongdoer critics" often include the people who seem to resist your help: the street person who struggles to get off drugs or the wayward youth bent on rebelling. The "self-important know-it-all" is more likely to be a colleague or leader who has decided to vent his or her misery on you. Both critics cause us great pain and great growth. As we surrender them to God, we'll taste and see what it means to have a reconciler's heart.

Jesus, who fielded criticism with great skill because he knew all men's hearts (Luke 5:22), warned us to be "as shrewd as snakes and as innocent as doves" (Matthew 10:16). You may need that reptilian shrewdness when people tell you *they* know what God wants you to know; when they insist you're wrong to spend your time helping abuse survivors or driving for Meals on Wheels. These well-intentioned prophets are sometimes adamant, crossing your spiritual boundaries as if they were the authoritative voice of God in your life. In truth, no one can climb up the mountain for you and listen for the gentle whisper of God (1 Kings 19:8,12). The best response is to ask your critics to pray for you.

ACCEPTING LESS-THAN-IDEAL CIRCUMSTANCES

Sometimes overt criticism isn't the problem; it's just that certain factors are working against our living out our purposes. There isn't enough time or money or personnel or education to move any farther down the road. Let's say you've worked hard on a project for several years and the fruit you had hoped for hasn't come. Is it time to quit? It might be (this is another place our partners can help us), but don't make the mistake of thinking that if God is in the purpose, he will make all the circumstances absolutely ideal. Thankfully, Priscilla didn't wait for stable connections in town before helping to start a church. Hannah didn't wait for adequate outside support to have a child (she'd been beaten up verbally by her husband's other wife and accused of drunkenness by a priest). And Mary Magdalene didn't wait for a credible reputation before she reported on the greatest event in history—the Resurrection. There will always be something or someone to distract you; that's a normal part of life.

We can find hope in realizing that ideal circumstances are not indicators of God's will. Many ventures we now consider "successful" began in situations a wise entrepreneur would have considered unsound and lacking in marketing opportunities. The door of purpose often opens in circumstances we would never otherwise choose. For example, Henrietta Mears was startled to think of leaving her secure job as a high-school principal and chemistry teacher in Minnesota to work at a church in Hollywood, California. "Henrietta came to the movie capital when it was just entering its hectic, carefree, and immoral apogee of fame. Sound movies were coming into their own and cowboys were galloping from Hollywood studios onto theater screens around the world, while heroes and starlets were setting the sex patterns for youth. The celluloid capital was not exactly the backside of a desert where a thoughtful Moses could have plenty of time to meditate on the fate of his people and to hear the call of God to deliver them. Could a lily grow in a quagmire? Could Hollywood produce anything spiritual? Henrietta Mears thought so."[2]

Sometimes you're following your purpose, but circumstances change and your life seems to drift. You have to start all over figuring out how to live out your purpose. With no history of illness, seminary graduate Toni Baldwin (mentioned in chapter 10) developed allergies to nearly everything in her environment and was forced to rely on tremendous amounts of medication. Finally, she was advised to seek relief by moving to Albuquerque, New Mexico, because of its high altitude. But what would she do there? She had served thirteen years on a church staff working with children, families, and adults. After that, she had worked for a publisher writing spiritual development materials. As Toni contemplated the move, she considered applying to become a chaplain in a hospital or hospice, but once she arrived in Albuquerque, reality set in. Those jobs had always been filled by retired males—not forty-ish females. She saw that she would have to become known and trusted in the local medical community before she could be considered for a chaplaincy. In the meantime, how would she make a living as well as live out the purposes God put within her?

Toni has experimented with this in her two current jobs: substitute teaching and writing case studies for a social services agency. "My purpose is to be involved in people's spiritual lives," she says. "At the moment, I cannot attach that purpose precisely to my jobs, but as I encounter children and their parents and rub shoulders with coworkers, I am somehow able to give them spiritual guidance and support. The surface tasks in teaching are classroom management and getting assignments done, but the essence is that you have six and a half hours a day with children. I can't just teach them data or skills; I must also do what God has called me to do: love, encourage, guide others."

On one long-term assignment, Toni befriended a student who was slower than the others and asked multiple questions about each assignment. In their frequent personal times together, this girl would tell Toni she was a good teacher because she took time to explain things. When Toni replied that this was a teacher's job, the little girl insisted that not every teacher thinks so.

Although Toni would prefer to be involved more directly in people's spiritual lives in a hospital or hospice setting, her purpose can't be squelched. She is building up a network of acquaintances in the healthcare field to prepare herself for a chaplaincy position. In the meantime, she lives out her purpose with teacher's aides and principals and—you may have picked up this theme already—with those whose minds and bodies aren't as quick as the next person's. "I've done some soul-searching and wondered realistically, *How is God going to use me with the gifts he's given me?* I know God's not wrong. I don't know exactly what the future will hold, but I'm positive God will use me."

When you're in the middle of a situation, don't consider less-than-ideal changes to be a signal to quit. Amy Carmichael (1867–1951) was a single woman missionary to India, who let God work out his purposes as she helped children and rescued temple prostitutes and established a home and school for them.[3] She urged us to accept what comes: "The best training is to learn to accept everything as it comes, as from Him whom our soul loves. The tests are always unexpected things, not great things that can be written up, but the common little rubs of life, silly little nothings, things you are ashamed of minding one scrap. They can knock a strong person over and lay him low. An inward grouse is a devastating thing."[4]

Women of purpose who stay on track are the ones who see their inward grouses as a signal to surrender one more troubling person or circumstance to God.

QUESTIONS TO PONDER OR DISCUSS

1. Have you let criticism keep you from pursuing God's purposes? If so, what do you think you need to know about criticism?
2. What less-than-ideal circumstances have you faced? Have they held you back or not?

EXPERIMENT IN LISTENING PRAYER

Ask God, *What do I need to know about the people who criticize me? Is there something legitimate I need to face?*

BIBLE PASSAGE TO CONTEMPLATE

> Let us throw off everything that hinders and the sin that so easily entangles, and let us run with perseverance the race marked out for us. Let us fix our eyes on Jesus, the author and perfecter of our faith, who for the joy set before him endured the cross, scorning its shame, and sat down at the right hand of the throne of God. (Hebrews 12:1-2)

SEVENTEEN

Pulling in the People You Love Without Turning Them Off

My friend Carrie* will find this book frustrating to read. She loves being a nurse and has explored ways to advance God's kingdom through her nursing skills, but she has given up all nursing now that she has three small children. After the first two were born, she continued to serve as a nurse for an annual week of camp with handicapped children (she took her babies and a teen friend to help). But she quit after several women at church chided her for not putting her family first.

When I saw her at a retreat recently, she seemed numb to the people around her. Then in the heat the next day, a woman with diabetes began to faint and Carrie intervened. We were so grateful Carrie knew what to do, and I told her, "It was good to see you in action."

She started to cry, "I want to be more useful to God." She went on to talk about the statistics regarding Down's syndrome children, and I could see that a hot flame of compassion still burned in this torn woman.

In this section on what it takes to stay on track, we're looking at snags encountered in pursuing purposes. One of them is how some women feel split these days between the families they love and the role they feel called

* not her real name

to fulfill in God's "family business." Following their purposes, they're afraid, might rankle their spouse, force their children to adjust, or upset the people at church. They decide it might be easier just to forget those God-given purposes.

Perhaps we're living in a backlash from the era when ministers and missionaries were taught to put all their time into ministry and "let God take care of their children." Has the pendulum swung, I wonder, to the place where women feel their only responsibility is to their family and they're forgetting the world that God so loved? Kari Torjesen Malcolm, missionary and conference speaker, writes about hearing a minister of a large church tell women that all their ministry must be performed in the home by loving their husbands and raising their children. "This man cites one passage in Titus and cancels all the other commandments given to men and women. By contrast, when Jesus gave his last orders to the men and women who were present at his ascension, [he named] the lost and hurting world, not [just] the home, [as] the focus of his Great Commission."[1]

One woman (who didn't wish to be identified) told me: "Because of my church's feelings about women not serving outside the home, I am rarely asked to express my spiritual gift as a Bible teacher. If my children don't behave perfectly, I am not asked to do anything at church. I don't like having my kids in the spotlight that way, so I teach Bible studies outside the church setting. It doesn't take away from being a parent. What I learn and teach constantly draws me back to being a more sensitive mom."

Neglecting children is wrong and neglecting ministry is wrong. We need to explore creative ways for families to minister together and support each other, rather than making women choose between either family or service to others. When Miriam Adeney was asked how she has answered both the call of God to use her gifts and the call of motherhood, she replied, "I don't see it as an either/or. For me it has not been an impossible problem because I have always been a thinker and a writer, and I would do that if I had twenty children."[2]

But how do we act on the God-given purposes in our lives and still be attentive, caring wives and mothers? First, we abandon the idea that God has designed life so family is separate from service and that the two must compete. In a speech at the 1997 Women's Ministries Symposium, Jill Briscoe talked about the fallacy of having a hierarchy of priorities, such as (1) God, (2) husband, (3) children, (4) church, and so on. Instead, she suggested, there's a hierarchy of principles—"God and his kingdom come first. God will tell you what is front and center today. Are you listening?"

If you're a praying person who listens to God and looks into the hearts of people around you, obeying the first and second commandments to love God and love others (Matthew 22:37-39), you'll know when to skip the day's entire to-do list and take *your kids* to the beach, take *yourself* to the beach, take *your Bible* to the beach, or take *your kids and your neighbor's lonely, autistic son* to the beach. If each day is about knowing and loving God, that day's activities will flow out of a divine common sense. In fact, you'll probably know beforehand because God will have been nudging you for quite some time.

WHOLE-LIFE MISSION

As you ponder what your mission statement might look like, consider putting it in terms of all the roles in your life: daughter, sister, parent, spouse, employee, neighbor, volunteer, or committee member. For example, Sandy Burgess is a wife and mother of three children, and her mission statement is "to bring others to a deeper understanding of Christ." She says, "I can do this by interacting with my kids, by teaching Bible studies and leading workshops."

While Sandy enjoys being a stay-at-home mom, she also works from her home about ten hours a week as a volunteer doing marketing and research for The Women's Ministries Institute. Occasionally, she runs their resource table at conferences. "I look at the research and marketing work I do as one way to fulfill my mission," says Sandy. "I wade through books and find out what will help others. When I display resources on a book table, I get excited about how these books will change people's lives. I'm constantly talking to my eight-year-old about her relationship with Christ and how it develops her as a person.

Susie's her best friend last week, not this week. We talk about how she can love Susie all the time because of who she is in Christ, not because of what Susie does."

Another way to state more completely who you are is suggested by Miriam Adeney in her book *A Time for Risking*. When someone asks, "What do you do?" include your purpose in your customary answer. For example, "I'm a homemaker, and I happen to be particularly interested in the development of children."[3] I might say, "I'm a writer, and I happen to be interested in social justice." Elaine Barsness might say, "I'm a nurse and also a foster parent." Evelyn Curtiss could say, "I own a bookstore and I happen to be interested in the economic development of south-central Los Angeles." By clearly stating who we are and who we are called to be, we reinforce our purposes to ourselves and we increase opportunities for reconciliation and networking.

BRINGING KIDS ON BOARD

With some creative rethinking, our kids can be our partners in ministry. Evelyn and Joe Curtiss combined family with ministry, and their three sons' involvement in ministry emerged. Mrs. Curtiss kept her boys with her in and around the bookstore when they were young. "When they started to school, they worked on Saturdays, first as chores, then we paid them," she says.

As soon as your kids are able to do *anything* involving your purposes, ask them to join you and tack on an ice-cream-cone treat to thank them. Our family has served together several times at the Samaritan Center, and my husband and kids know most of our homeless friends around town. In between their visits to the center, I keep them informed of clients' circumstances—jail, pregnancies, sicknesses, deaths. We've also volunteered at downtown shelters in several other cities, and we've worked as a family with Habitat for Humanity, finding a local group that allowed children under sixteen to help.

When I was assigned to write an article in which I had to interview ten poor people all over the country, I paid my teenagers to transcribe audio tapes of interviews with several Samaritan Center clients. I was careful to explain to

them the vision behind the task: "The readers of this article don't know anyone who's this bad off financially, so we're going to help them 'meet' these
people, hear their stories, and bond with them." I also explained that the clients
had shared their hearts, so we would pray for them at the dinner table and
honor them by keeping confidential what they revealed in the interview.

The purpose for bringing kids on board is not to keep ourselves from
feeling guilty for pursuing purpose-related tasks, but to teach children how to
minister to the needs of other people. By our example, we already show our
children how to shop, relax, and pray; we also need to show them how to serve.
If there is no way to involve your kids in your purposes, at least let them visit
the location where your purpose takes shape, so they can see what you do.

CHERISHING YOUR KIDS IN THE MIDST OF IT

It can be a delicate balance to love your kids thoroughly and pursue God's
purposes in life. Women who have experienced this challenge offer these ideas
to help.

Share the benefits with children. To keep them from turning off to
your purposes, let them participate in the joy as well as the work, says Evelyn
Curtiss. "We also involved them in other ministry aspects; my husband started
a boys club since we had boys. We also got away as a family. Every year we
took them on trips when we went to the Christian Booksellers Convention.
We didn't work all the time; we camped a lot, driving a twenty-one-foot trailer
to Chicago and Oklahoma and Mississippi."

Give them choices. In junior high, the Curtiss boys could choose if they
wanted to work at the bookstore as a paid job. "We told them not to feel guilty
if they didn't want to be involved, but they saw it as an advantage," says
Mrs. Curtiss. "Few African-American kids had families with a business, so we
hired them and many of their friends. They saw our hard work and heartbeat for giving to people in need." Today, her oldest son manages the second
Word of Life Bookstore, and her middle son works in insurance and securities but also does the bookkeeping for the stores. Her youngest son works in

the bookstore but seems to have Mrs. Curtiss's "entrepreneurship bug" as well as an interest in community development programs.

Schedule ministry around kids' important moments. Sandy Burgess and her husband, David, set a rule that they'll always be home for birthdays and anniversaries. Recently, Sandy arrived two days late at an important conference so she wouldn't miss being home for her daughter's birthday.

View caregivers as family members. If you need caregivers for your children, Miriam Adeney stresses, "Anytime a caregiver is employed, this person needs to become something of a family member, someone we would reach out and help. We need to support that person with child development materials and share insights on the child. We need to remember her on birthdays and holidays. We need to pray for her and build a relationship that will last after the employment ends."

This fits well with the age-old custom of children having a circle of caregivers comprised of parents, older siblings, and extended family members. Raising children in a single-family dwelling, isolated from the community, is a relatively new development in history. Women have been carrying babies on their backs for centuries, settling them in nearby hammocks, letting them know and be known in the community where they live.

SPOUSES AND FRIENDS

Sometimes you and your spouse may be united in purpose and work side by side, as are Rev. Joe and Evelyn Curtiss in the Word of Life Bookstore (which she manages) and the United Gospel Mission (which he manages), located next to each other in south-central Los Angeles. Or you may have the same purposes with different emphases. Elsie and Herb Purnell are both stateside missionaries, but Herb works in a missions-oriented teaching English as a second language program, while Elsie works with missionary kids and helps missionary families. Or you may support each other in changing focuses. Sheila Lichacz pursued her painting within the limitations of being an Air Force officer's wife; now that John is retired, he is her manager.

When there's dissonance with a spouse or close friend, ask yourself:

Does this discord tell me anything about my motives or character? Sometimes a spouse and friends distance themselves from our pursuit of purpose because they detect that our purpose is more about advancing ourselves than God's kingdom. Or they'll see how we can round up people to show kindness on overseas mission projects, but we're not able to be kind to family members. If they don't feel able to express this to us, they may use other reasons as a cover: "You're already too busy." "You need to pay more attention to me."

Is what I have in mind too disruptive for my life and the people around me? Maybe your purpose is on target, but the tasks you've chosen to express it intrude too much on family life or personal health. If so, you need to change or downsize tasks so that other people aren't paying for your ministry involvement.

On the other hand, this era of Supermom makes us reluctant to ask for help. The simple principle of "Say what you need" is difficult for us to embrace. One day when I was overcommitted with tasks, I stopped to water my garden and began wondering how JoeAnn Ballard survived with fifty-five foster kids over the years. Then it hit me: She asked them to help. I considered which of the day's tasks my kids could help with. I've learned to say to them, "I need… Can you help me?" From this they're learning not only new task skills but also the joy of a family working as a team.

Am I willing to support this person in the expression of their gifts and purpose? Perhaps you'll need to give support before you receive it. Do you go out of your way for your friends, spouse, or children? Do you listen long and hard to them? Look for ways to support them, and they'll usually become much more supportive of your purposes.

You may be looking at the above question and thinking, *All I've ever done is support his expression of gifts and purpose.* Sometimes when a spouse (or parent) has so much passion, it may seem as if there's no room for yours. You may be reluctant to seek God's purpose in your life because it would diminish your support of his. Consider that the opposite might be true. As you pursue your purposes in life, your interaction with God will deepen and you will grow as a person. Then you'll have more skills and wisdom with which to help.

Have I asked my spouse or friend to be my partner in ministry? Have you shared your deep sense of purpose, including the stories or statistics that break your heart? They may feel resistant to your purpose because they feel left out. "Let the peace of Christ keep you in tune with each other, in step with each other. None of this going off and doing your own thing" (Colossians 3:15, *The Message*).

Have I defined the ministry tasks too narrowly? An attitude popular today says that couples must work elbow-to-elbow on the same tasks in order to serve together. Christina Riccardi, who conducts neighborhood Bible studies and serves on the board of a crisis pregnancy center, wanted to work with her husband mentoring younger couples, but Charles wasn't interested. "I was disappointed, because I wanted to minister as a couple," says Christina. "A year later, one of the church leaders invited him to be on the worship team and he loves it. Many people tell him that he's a blessing on the team, but it was nothing I said that brought it about."

It's more important to listen to a husband's heart and listen to where he believes God is leading him than to create an idealized or romanticized picture of Christian service.

Is my spouse too insecure for me to venture out? If your husband is worried about your safety or your need for rest, discuss what can be done to alleviate that worry. Even if it seems silly to you, work out a way to address his concerns. If your husband is scared off by your passion, back off and talk calmly about the things that break your heart. Find a video to show him or read him a few paragraphs from literature that speaks to you. Let him see how God is working in you. Urge him to wrestle with God (not with you) over your involvement.

If your husband is afraid you'll outshine him, go slowly. Watch your heart, look at your options, care for him as a person. "The only thing that counts is faith expressing itself through love.... Serve one another in love.... If you keep on biting and devouring each other, watch out or you will be destroyed by each other" (Galatians 5:6,13,15).

Anytime a person you love seems to prevent you from fulfilling your purpose, remember that God is more concerned about your doing his will than you are. He will go before you and make a way for you to fulfill his purposes in some way.

CONSIDER THE ADVANTAGES

None of the above issues are easy to resolve, and it can be frustrating to feel you're switching gears, but consider that this is a good problem to have. It's not so bad to be surrounded by a family you love and also to have a purpose that is so terribly absorbing.

Family can enrich your purpose. Miriam Adeney is often asked if motherhood slowed her down in pursuing her doctorate degree. She says, "Of course. But it also draws you out on a million levels. Your children plug you into your community—the school system, the healthcare system, even your neighbors. The enrichment of having children is indescribable. You learn about passion and the fierceness of love."

Contrary to what some people may believe, a woman doesn't have to choose between having a purpose in life and being a faithful and fun-loving mom, wife, and friend. One of the best things we can contribute to the people we love is to be a woman who responds to the call of God. Through us, those we love experience the joy of following God and are often challenged to consider their own God-infused purposes.

QUESTIONS TO PONDER OR DISCUSS

Consider an area in which your relationship with family or friends seems to be conflicting with your purpose. Then answer these questions:

1. Does this discord reveal anything about your motives or character?
2. Is what you have in mind too disruptive for your life and the people around you?
3. Are you willing to support this person in the expression of their own gifts and purpose?
4. Have you asked this person to be your partner in ministry?

EXPERIMENT IN LISTENING PRAYER

Ask God, *How can I draw my friends and family into my purpose in life in some small way?*

BIBLE PASSAGE TO CONTEMPLATE

> Let the peace of Christ keep you in tune with each other, in step with each other. None of this going off and doing your own thing. (Colossians 3:15, *The Message*)

EIGHTEEN

MAKING THE TRADE-OFFS

How is it possible to devote our energies to God's purposes, meet all of our day-to-day responsibilities, and still have time to enjoy our lives? Even if you're an excellent manager of time, you'll explode if you try to have a purpose-full life, dazzling home, firm body, attractive appearance, fulfilling career, happy family—and ever go to the movies again. Something has to give—but what?

Anne Ortlund addressed this dilemma of staying focused twenty years ago in *Disciplines of a Beautiful Woman*: "You want to manage your time? You eliminate clutter and concentrate on your goals. You want to disciple? You eliminate crowds and concentrate on a few people."[1] Throughout the book, she focused on gradually cutting out nonessentials and focusing on what is most important.

TRADING TRIVIAL PURSUITS
FOR PURPOSEFUL ACTIVITY

This "eliminate and concentrate" principle means we cut less important activities—and maybe even some things that we love, but which crowd out the things we love more. "I know what it is to crumble up half an onion by hand and toss it into the fry pan, bits of husk and all, because I have a baby on one shoulder and can't manage a knife," writes Miriam Adeney. "I no longer play the violin, make yogurt or bake bread, sew most of my clothes, write many personal letters, or even talk much on the phone. My nonworking neighbors bowl, take fun classes, and work out at figure salons; I don't have those luxuries. My childless colleagues enjoy luncheons, parties, and pivotal committee meetings; I can't. That limits my decision-making power in the institutions where I teach. My yard has a very country look. Inevitably, when I'm pushing toward a deadline, one of my sons will shove a lima bean up his nose or a shampoo bottle down the toilet. And there are afternoons when I toss all priorities to the wind and sit down with a detective novel."[2]

Miriam's willingness to give up so much on a daily basis while still making time to occasionally read a detective novel tells us how puzzling it can be to identify what is frivolous in our lives. Walking on the beach or a solitary canyon road may be trivial or imperative, depending on what's going on in your life. If you are in dire need of renewal, if that walk is part of a regular reflection time, or if you walk to combine exercise and conversation with a friend you've missed, that walk is imperative. If your life is full of rest, leisure, and fun and you haven't thought about reconciliation or redemption for days, taking a walk may be trivial.

Another tricky thing about trade-offs is that they appear painful to onlookers, but they're not so painful to you when you're infused with purpose. You may raise your eyebrows at Miriam's saying she no longer plays the violin or bakes bread, but she has such a passion for cultural anthropology and teaching her students that these sacrifices don't hurt much. Besides, working within our purposes provides a lot of fun because we're sharing moments with God and our ministry partners. It can be so satisfying that we keep asking ourselves, *Hmmm…What else can I cut out?*

Certain activities fall into the trivial category in one season of life but may be imperative in another. Several personal and professional organizations have meant a great deal to me over the years and have helped me express my purposes. But now that I travel several weekends a year, I spend my weeknights driving my two teenagers to the places they need to be and making sure they have what they need. This is my pleasure for these years while they still live at home. If someone wants to meet me on a weeknight to talk about a problem, I have exactly one hour and twenty minutes at the coffee shop near my son's Explorer meeting. I wish I were more available, but at this season of my life I am not.

TRADING "HECTIC-ITY" FOR SIMPLICITY

A contemporary spin-off of Henry David Thoreau's famous quote, "The mass of men lead lives of quiet desperation,"[3] might be, "The mass of women lead lives of hectic busyness, desperate to go somewhere." Busyness makes us feel productive, which is highly valued in our culture. It makes us feel good to accomplish goals: finishing a term paper, running five errands in two hours, planning an outstanding women's luncheon at church. Yet our self-important busyness is often a pseudo-spirituality. "I'm just too busy to watch TV," we say with a saintly look about us. It's as if busyness is next to godliness.

Focusing on our purposes brings a natural sort of simplicity because we don't have as much time to collect "stuff" or to keep it clean and repaired. Author and former missionary Kari Torjesen Malcolm quotes a familiar Bible passage (Luke 3:11) with a contemporary twist: "'The man with two tunics should share with him who has none, and the one who has food should do the same.' But what should we do in a clothes crazy country like America? Perhaps we can start by not worrying about wearing the same outfit each time we go to church or to a party."[4]

As I've become more absorbed by God's purposes for me, I've quit thinking about clothes. I keep a list of outfits so I can dress in as few minutes as possible. I speak annually at an author's fair, and I had to laugh when I saw the pictures from the previous five years posted; there I was in my gray skirt and blue blouse year after year. It's still fun to pull together a new outfit, but now I get so much joy out of doing other things that the clothes issue has faded.

I've also given up being Supermom. I still want to give back to the organizations with which my kids are involved, so I do one simple task per year per organization. For Girl Scouts, I chaired the calendar sale, which lasted a few weeks and was over. For Boy Scouts, I was the secretary of the adult committee for many years, but it involved only one meeting a month. At school, I've served on the same committee for nine years, but I do little else at school.

Many resources are available to help us manage our time. As we use them to consciously plan how we will make time to fulfill our purposes, we'll want to include time for doing what I call, "serious nothing," a morning or a day or a week now and then where absolutely nothing is scheduled. Sometimes you'll end up getting the rest you need; other times you'll accomplish all the things you've been putting off. The goal is focus more than balance. Not every item gets equal time, but each item gets the attention it needs—exercise, house-keeping, and so on. That way, life does not slip away before we attempt to do the things God has put in our hearts.

TRADING SELF-FOCUS FOR A GOD FOCUS

Loving God and living in his purposes will make us radically different from our culture. Glenn Hinson, a professor of spirituality and church history, describes the heroes of church history, saying, "[They] are visionaries, people sometimes thought to be a bit loony by their contemporaries. When Christ finally captured him, Francis of Assisi (and Sister Clare of Assisi, not long after) gave up his affluent life, married Lady Poverty, and began doing all sorts of strange things—repairing churches, begging to care for the poor, kissing lepers, acting like a Jesus freak. They don't just dream dreams, they try to act them out. They make themselves fools for Christ's sake."[5]

In what ways are you and I called to be foolish or radical for Christ? We will be different from our culture, in which people "tend to worship their work, to work at their play, and to play at their worship. As a result, their meanings and values are distorted.... Their lifestyles resemble a cast of characters in search of a plot."[6] Is God calling you to quit putting so much time and energy into leisure? Is God calling you to set aside your love affair with your job? Is God calling you to make the words of your favorite hymn a life message or to spend an hour pouring your heart out to him? This is foolishly radical behavior.

As God has called me to focus on him, I've had to give up many self-involved, trivial habits. Ponder what habits God is calling you to abandon. Here are a few of mine to get you started:

Perfectionism. I've given up on appearing flawless in every area of life. On this side of heaven, I will not *always* be immaculately groomed, have a pencil-thin body, cook nutritious meals, be an avid Bible student, do a perfect job at work, pray for an hour a day, color coordinate my home furnishings, and wear a belt that matches my shoes and purse. While I wouldn't intentionally wear hosiery with a run in it, I don't worry if I get one. If there's a typo on my flier, the sun will still rise tomorrow morning. If the baseboards in my house aren't spic and span, I can still have a friend over. Our culture—so infatuated with efficiency and peak performance—cringes at the words of G. K. Chesterton, "If a thing is worth doing, it is worth doing badly."[7] As Jesus told Mary and Martha, "One thing is needful: and Mary hath chosen that good part, which shall not be taken away from her" (Luke 10:42, KJV). Perfectionism steals that one thing needful.

Creating a "statement of me." Before I determined to focus on purposeful activities, I spent a lot of time and energy creating an image. Finding just the right design for my checks or the right color of nail polish was a "statement of me," so I spent hours hunting and choosing. Now I find these things annoying because they cloud my life with a false sense of meaning and sprinkle clutter on my calendar.

I remind myself that, as a Christian, I'm committed to loving people and using things, instead of the reverse. My car or my house is never a statement of me. I invest time and effort in people instead of material items. Besides, when we focus on God's redemptive purposes, it generates such heat and light that we don't have time for these trivial matters. Simplicity in letter writing, home furnishings, and house cleaning becomes a downright necessity.

Focusing on personality instead of character. If I'm drifting through life, it's easy to be placated by entertaining speakers or celebrity trivia. But as my life with God becomes richer and I interact with God about my purposes, I see how much my character needs to grow. The heroes in life are the people who have died to themselves or showed mercy or reconciled with an enemy. As I focus less on personality, I accept the Christians I admire as people with flaws and troubles and a car that needs a paint job.

Christian women need and want something larger than themselves to live and die for. When this is lacking, the energy and passion intended to fulfill purpose gets hijacked, and we waste time brooding over who doesn't like us or why the pastor can't be more entertaining or sensitive. The best way to avoid pettiness in myself or a group of Christians is to focus on knowing Christ and making him known.

As inconsequentials fade, we have more time and presence of mind to converse with God about the things that break his heart. The apostle Paul focused on God with a single-mindedness. He said, "One thing I do: Forgetting what is behind and straining toward what is ahead, I press on toward the goal to win the prize for which God has called me heavenward in Christ Jesus" (Philippians 3:13-14). Paul left behind his esteemed reputation and powerful position, choosing instead to "know Christ and the power of his resurrection and the fellowship of sharing in his sufferings, becoming like him in his death" (Philippians 3:4-7,10). He threw away the "good life" and signed up for death to self.

By dying to ourselves, we join a long line of Christians through the ages who have stood in front of the burning bush and struggled to give themselves to the purposes of God. Also by dying to ourselves, we quite accidentally but happily find we are being conformed to the image of Christ as simple servants of the Most High God.

QUESTIONS TO PONDER OR DISCUSS

1. Which, if any of these things, are a problem for you: perfectionism, focusing on personality instead of character, creating a "statement of me"?
2. What area of your life is too cluttered: holidays, kids' activities, cleaning house, preparing meals, errand running? How does it distract you from your purpose?

EXPERIMENT IN LISTENING PRAYER

Ask God, *What will I have to lay aside to pursue my purposes? What is it I need to know about the busyness in my life?*

BIBLE PASSAGE TO CONTEMPLATE

Having a general structure for time helps us feel more hopeful about fulfilling the purposes God put within us:

> Live life, then, with a due sense of responsibility, not as men
> who do not know the meaning and purpose of life but as those
> who do. Make the best use of your time.... Don't be vague but
> firmly grasp what you know to be the will of the God.
> (Ephesians 5:15-17, Phillips)

NINETEEN

My Prayer for You

As I was sitting on the steep bank of a creek at a retreat center one day, I realized I needed to be praying for those who read my books. So as I write books and as they are distributed, I pray for you the reader. It's my delight to meet some of you when I speak at retreats.

In writing this book my prayer has been that our conversation together will change your life forever. As I look at the purposes stated on my whiteboard, I read the third one: "focusing the American church on the substance of God's mission instead of glitz." That's why I wrote this book. Today's women have more time, skills, and financial resources than ever before. What will we do with them? My hope and prayer is that we will not be satisfied with doing only what's expected of us, but that we will choose to participate in God's purposes: advancing the kingdom of God, demonstrating mercy and justice, reconciling people to God and each other.

Now that you have finished this book, my prayer for you is that you will persist in the journey. I pray that you will:

KEEP YOUR VISION INTACT...

Through hearing the tales of our sisters. When I finished reading the biography of Henrietta Mears on an airplane, I shut off my light, cried, and asked God to use me as he used her. The tales of our sisters who have followed their purposes in life inspire us and give us a vision of what God can do. Without such tales, my vision shrinks and I become overly concerned about the newest wrinkle in my face. The smudge in my carpet overwhelms me. But in focusing on the inspiring work of others, I'm prompted to resist the pull of my me-centeredness—for the good of my soul—to hear the struggles of clients at the Samaritan Center and to pray for the advancement of God's kingdom worldwide. Simply acquainting myself with the widow or single mother down the street opens up new windows and increases my vision.

Through giving time to what renews you. Our purposes need to be fed the way lakes are restocked with fish. Figure out what feeds you as a person and make a holy habit of doing these things—going to a concert, reading a novel, leafing through a book of art or hiking through the woods. JoeAnn Ballard, who is so infused with the purpose of coming alongside others, finds renewal in fishing—a solitary activity. "When I get my fishing pole, my husband says, 'I know you're up to something.' I do that four or five times a year. It feels like work to me because it's 'vision time.'"

The activities that feed your *being* also feed the fire of your *doing*. The activity may seem unrelated to your purpose, but you return from it refreshed. After working all day and thinking hard, I devote my waning energy to my exercise workout. My thoughts quiet as my body imitates the movements on the television screen. This is when I get fresh ideas about writing, speaking, and being the person I'm called to be in my relationships. While my mind is quieted, it seems to talk to my spirit and confer with my imagination, then they all send me a message. Sometimes feelings I've buried all day surface, and I sob as I punch the air. At the close of my workout I take my shower with a sense of renewal, having spent my agonies and uncovered new ideas.

Through your finding "thin" places. Author and translator Evelyn Underhill tells a story about a woman who returned to the mainland of Scotland after a visit to the island of Iona, where Columba and his monks had lived in the sixth century. She spoke to a gardener one day about the beauties of the island. He said, "Yes, Mum, Iona's a very thin place." Asked what he meant by that remark, he added, "Well, on Iona, Mum, there's a very little between you and God."[1]

If you pursue the purpose God has put within you, your head will be swirling. Treat yourself to frequent journeys to your "thin places." The ground is not more sacred there than elsewhere, but you have trained your spirit to connect quickly with God there. Go as regularly as you can. Also, cultivate several thin places close to your home and workplace. In the middle of the city, find the spot—perhaps a bench or café (mine was a cemetery)—that becomes a thin place for you. In a house full of preschoolers, hide a few favorite books behind the couch and know that a thin place awaits, where you and God can sort out more questions regarding the passion he's put within you.

I pray also that you will:

GUARD YOUR HEART

It doesn't take much success for others to think you're successful, and they soon equate the success with you instead of with God. If you're not careful, you may begin to wonder why everyone doesn't see how wonderful you are. When you start "owning" the purpose, you're in trouble. It may be good that the "stone doesn't always know what ripples it has caused in the pond whose surface it impacts."[2]

Your job is not to be a success, but to stay tied to the heart of God. Success must become a nonissue. We are faithful. If people notice, fine. If they don't, that's fine too. One warning sign that success is tainting our character and purpose in life is when we find ourselves seeking greater influence. Are you upset because the program isn't big enough or because not enough people attend? It's difficult to declare once and for all that the wideness of our influence is God's business, not mine. "Greatness…appears to be not so much a certain size as a certain quality of human lives. It may be present in lives whose range is very small."[3]

Another warning sign is when we consider changing direction to achieve greater success. A Bible teacher once confided in me that she was tempted to teach only New Testament studies because the classes were better attended than Old Testament studies. But she respected the whole counsel of God and would continue to move back and forth. God calls us to participate in a cause that breaks our heart, not one that draws a crowd. God gave Jeremiah the purpose of preaching to and handholding a nation of losers who wouldn't listen to him. Then Judah was captured by Babylon, and Jeremiah went with Judah into captivity, weeping with them and encouraging them. His was not an upwardly mobile career, but it was God's career for him.

You may be called to some causes that appear hopeless, but you are nevertheless called to them. Václav Havel, philosopher and president of the Czech Republic—thus well acquainted with issues of hopelessness—talked about hope being "an ability to work for something because it is good, not just because it stands a chance to succeed."[4]

Your "career" or "cause" may not appear successful. Few of the drug addicts you help may get—or remain—clean. The relatives of patients in the hospice in which you volunteer may discount your help. No one may sign up to be a missionary after you work hard on a missions fair. Your calling is not dependent on success, but on the loving, nurturing relationship you have with God. You will not find meaning in your service. Instead, your service will exhaust you, tempt you, and force you to stay awake at night. Your meaning will come from Christ and the love relationship you have with the Father.

The principle of guarding your heart (Proverbs 4:23-25) involves using certain habits or disciplines to help us let go of our drive for success, a little at a time. You may think you don't have this problem, but beware. It's woven into the fabric of our culture. Here are some ideas to consider:

Give away power. Are you willing to give referrals, time, ideas, and honor to people pursuing the same purpose in different ways (in other words, helping the "competition")? Are you partnering with others? Are you discipling someone else in fulfilling the same purpose? It's interesting to see how churches that plant a new work from their membership usually recover well from the loss of members. Their giving spirit is evident and people are drawn to it.

Don't get sidetracked from your mission. The applause of planning a successful event or achieving a goal can dull you and distract you from the purpose in your heart. Success can make you unwilling to move on to the next task out of fear it won't be as successful. I heard Pulitzer Prize–winning author Annie Dillard explain that, after she won this prestigious prize for

Pilgrim at Tinker Creek at a relatively young age, she moved to Washington state to get as far away as she could from New York City, the center of publishing. Why? She knew that in New York she would be a celebrity and lose a sense of herself and her mission. Unless you're focused, your time will be co-opted by well-intentioned people who ask you to do too many wonderful things not associated with your purpose.

Beware of compliments. Most of us struggle to accept them, but the paradox is that we also begin to believe them and focus on our accomplishments. Jesus told the elated disciples to focus on their connection with God, not their dazzling miracles (Luke 10:17,20), and that caution stands true for our less-than-miraculous deeds. If you want to use a compliment constructively, ask compliment-givers what specifically helped them. Draw out their story. This helps you know how to better serve others, because it gives you concrete feedback.

Don't take glory seriously. Being featured or honored is fun, but it's short-lived. A few days after a convention in which my picture was splashed across a huge pane of translucent glass for thousands to see, I sat hunched under my dining room table cleaning spots out of the carpet. *If they could see me now!* I thought. Enjoy these times, but always remember the One whose esteem you already have.

Admit there are things you don't know or understand. Just when you're convinced you are brilliant and you do know which end is up, it's delightful and humbling to watch someone else succeed in fixing your desk chair or finding the item you're sure you lost. There is so much that each of us can't do and don't know.

And last, I pray that you will:

LET SUFFERING CREATE DEPTH

Suffering—illness, broken relationships, financial hardships—smacks of anything but success and achievement. No one would seek such things, but they happen and they can—if we cooperate with God—create in us a depth that is unusual. Missionary Amy Carmichael reminded herself and others: "When heaven is about to confer a great office on a man, it always first exercises his mind and soul with suffering, and his body with hunger, and exposes him to extreme poverty, and boggles all his undertakings. By these means it stimulates his mind, hardens his nature, and enables him to acts otherwise not possible to him."[5]

When we have a heart for God, whatever thwarts us can become what teaches us to know and love God. Our struggles refine us. When I teach at retreats, women say to me (too often), "This sounds terrible, but I'm glad you've been through so much so you can share it with us." Part of me wants to scream, but the truth is that my struggles have taught me the importance of having an authentic relationship with God and that has become a life message for me. None of us would sign up for pain or scarcity or neediness, but these things prepare us for something important if we embrace God in the midst of them.

Too often we let suffering become a show-stopper. If our suffering has nothing to do with our purposes, we especially can't figure out how it could be of any help. Mature Christians report that suffering reshapes, molds, and deepens not only us, but our purposes in life. It nearly always expands our ministry in some way.

A prime example is artist Sheila Lichacz. For three decades, she has fought the growth of benign but life-threatening tumors in her head. She has survived ten surgeries to remove more than seventeen brain tumors. One was so close to her optic nerve that they thought she would lose her eyesight, but she did not. When I asked her how these tumors have affected her art, Sheila said, "The reason my work is so spiritual is that without faith I would never have survived. I have been in hospitals too long not to understand what is really important."

Sheila has been told many times she will not survive an operation, and at this writing she has three tumors in her head. These tumors, she says, along with the shards of pottery from the Rio Santa Maria in Panama, have been the tools God has used to reshape and salvage her life. "They have made me fearless," she told me. The result of this shaping has been that art critics (who usually do not prefer works with religious themes) have proclaimed her work to be full of faith and hope.

If we value our suffering and let it reshape us, our purpose can be forged even stronger as we choose peacefulness and hope over bitterness and despair. The psalmists gave us words for this process, including these words from David: "Though I walk in the midst of trouble, you preserve my life; you stretch out your hand against the anger of my foes, with your right hand you save me. The LORD will fulfill his *purpose* for me; your love, O LORD, endures forever— do not abandon the works of your hands" (Psalm 138:7-8, emphasis added).

The psalmist's plea was, of course, a moot point. God will not abandon us, the work of his hands. He asks that each of us cooperate with the force of his fingers and the nudges of his voice to become vessels he can use.

As you ponder what purpose looks like in your life, make a list of what you think God is calling you to do after reading this book. As you pray and ponder, review the parts of the book that spoke to you most clearly. Wrestle with them until God's will becomes clear, until your heart is thoroughly broken with the things that break the heart of God and until a way is made clear to fulfill the purposes God has given you. I will be praying that you have clarity to see God's purposes and the courage to grasp them. I will be praying that you:

- Keep your vision intact.
- Guard your heart.
- Let suffering create depth.

Feel free to let me know how the journey is going by writing to me:

Jan Johnson
c/o WaterBrook Press
5446 North Academy, Suite 200
Colorado Springs, CO 80918

QUESTIONS TO PONDER OR DISCUSS

1. Where are you most likely to hear encouraging tales of your sisters?
2. What kinds of things do you need to do to keep the lake of your soul stocked with fish?
3. Where are your "thin places"?

EXPERIMENT IN LISTENING PRAYER

On a regular basis for the rest of your life, ask God, *Show me how to become a person of vision.*

BIBLE PASSAGE TO CONTEMPLATE

Read this passage aloud, replacing the blanks with your name:

> My purpose is that _____ may be encouraged in heart
> and united in love, so that _____ may have the full riches
> of complete understanding, in order that _____ may
> know the mystery of God, namely, Christ, in whom are hidden
> all the treasures of wisdom and knowledge. (Colossians 2:2-3)

CELEBRATE IN PRAYER

Enjoy applying this prayer of Augustine to your own experience:

> Thou didst call, and shout, and burst my deafness. Thou didst
> flash, shine, and scatter my blindness. Thou didst breath odors,
> and I drew in breath, and pant for Thee. I tasted, and I hunger
> and thirst for Thee. Thou didst touch me, and I am on fire for
> Thy peace.[6]

APPENDIX

SEEKING BIBLICAL DIRECTION

As you read this book and consider what living a purpose-full life means for you, you may enjoy a more in-depth study of the Bible passages mentioned. Here are some questions to help you explore God's purposes for your life.

CHAPTER 1: HUNGRY FOR PURPOSE

Read Acts 17:27-28.

1. What phrases in this passage describe people's longing for God?
2. In what ways do people *seek* God, *reach out* to God, and *find* God?
3. What evidence do you see in the people around you of a longing for something (or Someone) bigger than themselves?
4. In what circumstances are you most sure of this truth: "In him we live and move and have our being"?
5. When, if ever, have you experienced a sense of lostness from being outside a relationship with God or existing outside his purposes?

Read Psalm 63.

6. What activities of this psalmist's body indicate his longing for God?
7. How is the psalmist hungry for God's justice to be worked out?
8. In what instances are you as thirsty for God as the psalmist? (If you can't think of any, describe what instances you can imagine that would make you thirsty for God.)

9.   In what ways have you tried to find meaning and purpose apart from God (or with God added on only as a frill, not the core motivation)?

10.   What would it look like for you to be more closely tied to the heart of God?

CHAPTER 2: WORKING FROM THE HEART

1.   Today's passage is often referred to as Jesus' graduate sermon. He was coming back to his hometown much like seminary graduates return to their home churches to preach a sermon. The hometown crowd judges severely its own, and the graduates are usually eager to please. Consider what topic you think Jesus would want to highlight on this important occasion.

Read Luke 4:16-22.

2.   Why would such a sermon be unpopular among Jews? (Remember that many Jews considered those who were physically handicapped to have missed the blessing of God.)

3.   The opening phrase, "The Spirit of the Lord is on me, because he has anointed me to…" indicates that this sermon was personal. It was about Jesus' purposes here on earth. List those purposes.

4.   In what ways do you see Christians today fulfilling those same purposes?

5.   What words or phrases in this passage indicate that Jesus didn't pull these purposes out of the air, but they issued from his long love relationship with the Father?

Read Luke 4:23-30.

6.   Why would Jesus' references to the widow of Zarephath and Naaman the Syrian have alienated this synagogue-going, ethno-centric Jewish audience?

7.   How did Jesus' sermon serve God's global purposes of reconciling the world to himself and advancing his kingdom here on earth?

8. When has the Christian message seemed radically different from the world around you?

9. Is anyone you know impoverished in some way, imprisoned in some way, blind in some way, oppressed in some way?

10. What does a hurting world around you need to know most about God?

CHAPTER 3: MISCONCEPTIONS ABOUT PURPOSE

Read 2 Kings 4:38-41 and 6:1-7.

1. How did the prophet Elisha help the company of prophets whom he mentored?

Read 1 Kings 18:16-39.

2. What miracle did Elijah perform in this passage?

3. In what ways did these two prophets differ in their ministries? In terms of drama? In their involvement of other people?

4. How might someone who favors the dramatic, introverted style of Elijah discount the ministry of Elisha?

5. How might someone who favors the people-oriented style of Elisha criticize the ministry of Elijah?

6. Which prophet's ministry does your service resemble? Are your purpose-oriented tasks dramatic or everyday? Solitary or connected with people?

7. How are you sometimes drawn into thinking that others' service isn't as effective as yours?

8. Do you ever discount the effectiveness of the kind of service you're drawn to? (For example, perhaps ministry to children doesn't seem as important as helping the homeless.) If so, how?

9. Elijah and Elisha had many things in common: They faithfully fulfilled the ministry to which they were called, and they were loyal to God at great cost to themselves. In what way does the type of ministry to which you're drawn demand faithfulness and integrity?

10. Consider whose service in the Bible you admire (the woman in Proverbs 31; Esther; Mary, the mother of Jesus). What does that tell you about yourself and your service?

CHAPTER 4: THE FEMININE EDGE OF PURPOSE

Read 1 Samuel 2:1-8.

1. After God gave a son to Hannah, who had been childless, she prayed. What emotions do you find recorded in this prayer?
2. What ideas did Hannah include in her prayer? Are any of them unexpected to you?
3. In what way had God redeemed Hannah's life? (Keep in mind a woman's chief purpose in ancient cultures.)
4. For a childless woman to have a son was a great reversal. What other great reversals are included in Hannah's prayer?
5. Try to see with God's eyes and name some great reversals you think he would like to see occur.
6. It's extraordinary that this woman thought about the state of others. Think of something good that happened to you recently. How did it benefit others too?
7. Hannah cared about people she didn't even know and seemed to see herself as a member of a global village under God's rule. What godly purposes (such as justice or mercy) would you like to see fulfilled in other parts of the world?

Read Luke 1:46-55.

8. In what ways does Mary's song (also related to the birth of a child) resemble Hannah's song?
9. If you were to set these verses to music, which phrases would you choose for the most passionate portions of the song?
10. In what ways do these two passages inspire you to imitate Hannah or Mary?

CHAPTER 5: LINKING UP WITH GOD'S PURPOSES

Read Genesis 12:1-3; 22:15-18; 26:1-5.

1. What promises did God make to Abraham?

2. Imagine you are Sarah. Explain how these promises—God's covenant—answer your greatest hopes.

3. How did God intend for his covenant with Abraham to affect the entire world?

Read Isaiah 51:4-5; Galatians 3:8.

4. Think about Old Testament history. In what ways did the nation of Israel bless the world's peoples?

5. Think about the New Testament and your own life. In what ways has Israel blessed the world?

6. In what ways does God bless Christians (spiritually, financially, intellectually) so they can bless others on the earth?

7. When have you had a sense of using the resources God has given you—incredible love, increased understanding, material goods—to be a blessing to others?

Read Jeremiah 4:1-2.

8. What did God command Israel to do in order to fulfill its role of becoming a blessing to the nations?

9. What idols do you need to let go of in order to be a blessing to other people on the earth and in our neighborhood?

Read 1 John 3:16-20; Ephesians 2:10.

10. How do you believe God is calling you to be a blessing to others?

CHAPTER 6: LOOKING FOR CLUES

Read 2 Corinthians 1:3-7.

1. How readily do you call God "the Father of compassion and the God of all comfort" (verse 3)?

2. How would you define the "sufferings of Christ" (verse 5)?

3. How does God comfort people in their troubles?
4. What phrase or song (or other expression) embodies the comfort of Christ for you?
5. Describe a time when you received the comfort of Christ.
6. For what issues do you still need the comfort of Christ?
7. Based on what you know of Scripture, what thoughts or feelings or attitudes are part of the "comfort of Christ"?
8. Describe a time when you passed on the comfort of Christ to someone else. (If you can't think of a time, describe how you think it would work.)
9. Have your sufferings produced "patient endurance" or bitter despair? Why?
10. What visual illustration would you use to describe the truths in this passage?

CHAPTER 7: THE STAGES OF DISCOVERY

Read Matthew 25:14-30.

1. What criteria did the man use for how many talents he gave each servant?
2. What character qualities did the first two servants display in putting their money to work right away?
3. In what practical ways do you—or could you—display those same character qualities in your life?
4. What, if any, inclinations or holy desires have you buried and might need to dig up to explore your purposes in life?
5. What were the master's responses to the first two servants?
6. How does the one-talent servant's wrong assumption compare to our assumptions about God?
7. What emotion did he feel toward his master?
8. What attitudes and emotions is this parable recommending that we have toward God?

9. What does the master's incremental method of talent giving tell us about how much ability or understanding is given at one time?

10. This passage speaks to those who want to instantly "be in charge of many things" and those who are afraid to use the desires and bent God has given them. Which of these describes your tendencies? What is God saying to you?

CHAPTER 8: STATING YOUR MISSION

Read 1 Samuel 25:2-9.

1. What reward did David hope to receive for protecting Nabal's shepherds and sheep?

Read 1 Samuel 25:10-17.

2. What was Nabal's response (see the summary in verse 14), and how did David react to it?

3. What did Nabal's servants do to act as peacemakers?

Read 1 Samuel 25:18-31.

4. What specific things did Abigail do and say to further the cause of peace?

5. When you're making peace among others, which of Abigail's attitudes do you find most difficult to emulate: appealing without begging; appealing to the conscience not the emotions; using common sense to show that peace is the most favorable choice for all?

Read 1 Samuel 25:32-42.

6. What did David say to indicate that he knew Abigail saved him from his own misguided violence?

7. Abigail aligned herself with the godly values of peace and reconciliation. What ungodly values *could* she have had in this complex situation?

8. When we get in highly emotional, complex situations, how can we stay focused on kingdom values such as love, joy, peace, patience, and self-control?

9.   What situation are you currently experiencing that requires a big-picture thinker—one who can project a peaceful, positive outcome and appeal to others to do what is best?

10. Consider your purposes in life; in what way are they connected to reconciling people to Christ, to others, or to yourself?

CHAPTER 9: A HEART FOR GOD

Read Mark 1:29-38.

1.   List the various tasks Jesus did on the day described in this passage. Which would you have found most exciting? Most exhausting?

2.   Notice the contrast in verses 33-35: the whole town gathered at the door versus Jesus going off to a solitary place. From what you know of Scripture and from the passage, what would you imagine Jesus prayed about in this solitary place?

3.   What does this contrasting behavior—radical service and radical aloneness with God—tell us about the current idea that some of us are like Mary and others are like her sister, Martha?

4.   Which are you more in need of—radical aloneness or radical service?

5.   Do you find the thing you need more of (question 4) to be an easy or difficult thing?

6.   In verse 38, Jesus gives one of his several purpose-in-life statements. Regarding your life, what phrase would you state before, "That is why I have come"?

7.   Why is it important for radical servants of God to be alone with God?

8.   Why is it important for those who are more devotional (and perhaps solitary) in nature to be involved in gritty service?

9.   What kind of "work" gets done in prayer?

10. In what ways is God calling you to reflect your purposes in life both in service and in solitary moments with him?

CHAPTER 10: NOT ENOUGH CONFIDENCE ...TOO MUCH CONFIDENCE

Read Isaiah 55:5; Lamentations 4:1-2.

1. What positive ways does God describe humans on earth?
2. What do you like or dislike about the image used by the writer of Lamentations—that we are pots of clay in the Father's hands?

Read Zephaniah 3:17.

3. Besides being treasures and being pliable, what else does Scripture tell us about how God views us?
4. Self-doubt makes us disbelieve the above scriptural truths. When do you struggle most with this?
5. Which of these word pictures is easiest for you to envision: you dressed in splendor, you as lustrous gold, you as a ruby or diamond, you as a pot of clay in God's hands, you being loved and sung over by the Father?
6. What benefits result from this God-centered self-worth?
7. One benefit of God-centered self-worth is the freedom and ability to obey Philippians 2:3-4. Read that passage now and notice the more specific benefits named there.
8. Why are humility and others-centeredness easier when you have a correct vision of how loved and valued you are by God?
9. Why do people with this God-centered self-worth make more effective servants?
10. In what places of service do you need an absolute sense of God's regard for you?

CHAPTER 11: NURTURING GOD-EMPOWERED PASSION

Read Exodus 1:15-21.

1. What civil disobedience did the Hebrew midwives commit?
2. What was their primary motivation in doing so?

3. The Hebrew midwives risked the Pharaoh's disapproval. When have you risked the disapproval of someone important to do what you believed God was calling you to do?

4. If you had been the mother or sister of Shiprah or Puah, would you have advised them to take these work-related risks? Why or why not?

5. What do you think is the difference between wise risk taking and reckless risk taking?

6. What woman have you known who has taken a wise risk?

7. In what ways did God reward the midwives for their obedience to him?

8. In what way did these midwives participate in the redemption and liberation of Israel?

9. What wise (but still scary) risks would you need to take if you pursued more diligently the purposes in life you believe God has laid before you?

10. Who could be your partner in these risks (as Shiprah and Puah were partners)?

CHAPTER 12: EVEN THE LONE RANGER HAD A SIDEKICK

Read Mark 14:32-42.

1. This passage describes when Jesus prayed in the Garden of Gethsemane before his death. What did he request of his three friends?

2. What does it mean to "stay here and keep watch" with a friend who's in trouble?

3. What sort of friends or partners do you need to "stay here and keep watch" as you pursue your purposes in life?

4. What can we learn from Jesus asking these three friends for help?

5. How well did Jesus' three friends succeed in doing what he asked?

6. What does this tell us about the expectations we have of our friends and partners?

7. In what ways do we fall asleep on each other when our purposes in life become perplexing?

8. Who are the people who seem interested and excited about what God is doing in your life?

Read James 5:16; Galatians 6:1-5.

9. What kinds of activities are involved when you "stay here and keep watch" with a family member or friend who is trying to follow God's purposes in life?

10. For whom are you serving as a partner for their purposes in life?

CHAPTER 13: DREAMING IN PURPOSEFUL WAYS

Read Jeremiah 32:39.

1. This verse was prophesied to the Israelites in captivity because they had tried to serve both God and idols. What did the phrase "single-ness of heart and action" mean for them?

2. What did God say would be the results of their singleness of heart and action?

3. The captivity of the Jews limited their service to God. What limitations do you face in your service to God?

4. What additional skills—dreaming, resilience, decision making—do you need in order to serve with singleness of heart? Write a few sentences about how being faithful in learning them would help you be faithful to God's efforts to work out his purposes in you (see Luke 16:10).

Read Luke 16:13-15.

5. What did the Pharisees love that kept them from serving God with a single focus?

6. How did this distraction taint their opinions and decisions (verse 14)?

7. The Pharisees "justif[ied] [them]selves in the eyes of men." How does self-justification keep us from learning from our failures?

8. If Jesus were addressing the religious people of today, what things might he say we try to serve in addition to God?

9. What is most distracting to you in serving God?

Read Mark 10:17-22.

10. Jesus looked at the rich young ruler and loved him even as he asked him to give up what he loved most—his riches. Envision God's looking at you and loving you. Imagine him also asking you to give up the things that keep you from having a singleness of heart.

CHAPTER 14: BRING YOUR BROKENNESS TO GOD

Read Luke 15:1-7.

1. What prompted Jesus to tell this parable?

2. Shepherds did not, as a rule, leave sheep in the open country; they put them in a sheepfold before leaving them. What does this tell you about the shepherd, the sheep, and the situation in which the shepherd left them?

3. What is the attitude of the shepherd toward the lost sheep who was stubborn or perhaps inattentive?

4. How do you imagine God feels toward you when you are rebellious or perhaps inattentive?

5. When have you, like this one-hundredth sheep, been rescued by God?

6. When that happened, did you beat yourself up or did you see yourself as the cause of a big party (verse 7)?

7. How does this treasured, redeemed image of ourselves speak to the self-doubt, despair, and hopelessness we sometimes experience?

8. How does it speak to the perfectionistic person who feels the need to prove herself and please others at all times?

Read Matthew 11:28-29.

9. What is God's will for us when we're weary and burdened?
10. What do these two verses say about rest? Why is that important for you?

CHAPTER 15: WHEN YOU FEEL LIKE QUITTING

Read Ruth 1:1-22.

1. List the tragic circumstances that Ruth, Naomi, and Orpah had to endure (verses 1-7).
2. If you were moving to a foreign land with only an older woman as a companion (as Ruth did), what would have scared you most?
3. Why do you think these two young women (Orpah and Ruth) were so willing to move to a foreign country?
4. What do you see at work in Ruth's heart in her plea to go with Naomi (verses 16-17)?
5. When has a role model given you the courage to do something difficult or scary?
6. Later, Ruth gleaned from the fields so she and Naomi could have something to eat (2:2-23). What does this tell you about perseverance?
7. What are your greatest struggles with perseverance? (For example, not expecting problems to occur or unwillingness to work hard.)

Read Philippians 4:8.

8. Meditate on what you've just read. What is true, noble, right, pure, lovely, or admirable about the things God is calling you to do?
9. In view of the passages you've read, what would you say are the keys to having a spirit of determination?
10. Write a prayer asking God for courage to persevere in your purposes in life.

CHAPTER 16: MOVING AROUND THE OBSTACLES

Read Luke 15:11-32.

1. Look at this passage through the eyes of the father. List all the possible reactions he did not choose in the events described in verses 11-19.

2. When someone does wrong, in what ways does our reaction tend to differ from the father's?

3. Write a sentence describing how the father may have felt when his younger son was off wasting his life. When have you felt this way?

4. Now examine what the father did do (verses 20-24). What traits are required to be able to welcome someone who has reversed himself?

5. Which son do you resemble: the penitent wrongdoer or the irritated but dutiful good-deed-doer? Think of an example from your life that shows this.

6. Describe the response of the father to the older son.

7. Meditate on the words of the father: "You are always with me, and everything I have is yours" (verse 31). In what situation in your life do you need to hear those words from God?

8. Is there someone you resent for one of the following reasons:
    * Success and achievement come easily to them.
    * People forgive them too easily.
    * They always seem to come out on top.

Read Matthew 7:1.

9. In this verse the Greek word for "judge" is the one that means "condemn." In other passages, we're urged to judge in the sense of discerning (see Luke 5:22; Matthew 10:16). In what situations do you need to be discerning but not condemning?

10. Who in your life is an obstacle to your moving forward in God's plan? How do you believe God wants you to view this person?

Chapter 17: Pulling in the People You Love Without Turning Them Off

Read Galatians 5:1-26.

1. This chapter begins by warning against a legalistic obedience that forces Christians to obey laws such as circumcision. Paul contrasts the role of the Spirit (mentioned five times) with the role of the law. How would you describe the role of the Spirit?

2. What are the results of living by the Spirit?

3. Paul says the law is summed up in a single command: "Love your neighbor as yourself." What opposite behavior is mentioned in this passage?

4. What role does the leading of the Spirit play in the turmoil women may feel between the things God calls them to do and the needs of the people they love?

5. How does paying attention to the needs of the people we love equip us for service?

6. Which items listed in verses 19-21 can occur in someone who desperately wants to serve God?

7. Describe how God might work out this verse in your life: "But do not use your freedom to indulge the sinful nature; rather, serve one another in love" (verse 13).

8. In what ways do we make it difficult to partner with friends and family? For example, defining ministry tasks too narrowly (couples *must* serve together, children cannot be involved), not giving others choices or rewards, or forgetting to explain your vision to them.

9. In what ways have you encouraged the people you love (friends, spouse, children, coworkers) to be your partners in ministry?

10. If conflicts have occurred with others, how has this prompted you to change your attitude about getting your own way or to practice showing tenderness of spirit?

CHAPTER 18: MAKING THE TRADE-OFFS

Read Luke 10:38-42.
1. What did Martha do right? How did it go wrong?
2. Mary's choice to sit at Jesus' feet and listen to him teach was a radical action in her day. In what radical way is God asking you to pay attention to him?
3. Mary's housekeeping or cooking might not have been as exemplary as Martha's. How do you feel when people find your work lacking?

Read Philippians 3:1-15.
4. What important and prestigious things did Paul lay aside (verses 4-6)?
5. What did Paul give as the reason for laying aside these things?
6. What words of focus and determination do you find in this chapter?
7. How does a focused life lead you away from chaos and into simplicity?
8. In what way does a simple, focused life require death to self?
9. What has been "to your profit" that you could now "consider loss for the sake of Christ" (verse 7)?
10. What verse in these passages contains a motto that would be perfect for a superwoman of our time?

CHAPTER 19: MY PRAYER FOR YOU

Read Luke 10:17-20.
1. Describe a time when you've had a spiritual experience (an answered prayer, a helpful person arriving just when needed). How did you feel about it? Did you tell others?
2. Why do you think the disciples were so filled with joy?
3. How did Jesus' answer put everything in the proper perspective?

4. What do you think Jesus meant by saying, "Rejoice that your names are written in heaven"?

5. Write a sentence here to thank God for salvation and for a future of fellowship with him.

6. How does the satisfaction you expressed in the above sentence differ from the self-focus of spiritual highs and achievements?

Read Psalm 138:7-8.

7. Of the actions attributed to God in this passage, which ones do you particularly need?

8. When, if ever, do you fear that God will abandon the purposes he's given you?

Read Psalm 30.

9. In this psalm, David has succeeded over his enemy. Find all the places in which David recounted what God did.

10. Which of these items could you easily thank God for as well?

NOTES

Chapter 1: Hungry for Purpose

1. "Ain't Got No Satisfaction: Working Women," *Psychology Today*, July-August 1993, 18.
2. According to Richard Hokenson, chief economist for Donaldson, Lufkin & Jenrette Securities in New York. Hokenson's original study was released in October 1993, republished in *U.S. Economic Outlook* on 4 March 1994, and then featured by *Barron's* (the Dow Jones business and financial newspaper) on 21 March 1994.
3. Leith Anderson, "Clocking Out: Women Are Choosing to Leave the Work Force in Increasing Numbers," *Christianity Today*, 12 September 1994, 30.
4. Katherine T. Beddingfield et al. "20 Hot Job Tracks," *U.S. News & World Report*, 28 October 1996, 92.
5. Press release from Amy Watson, Coach U., Profusion Communications, undated.
6. Michael G. Wagner, "Did Politics Kill Farm-Worker Aid Bill? Elizabeth Dole Plan Thwarted by White House, Ex-Aides Say," *Sacramento Bee,* 24 September 1992.
7. Frank Laubach, *Man of Prayer: The Heritage Collection* (Syracuse, N.Y.: Laubach Literacy International, 1990), 22.
8. This chart is adapted from Marsha Sinetar, "The Three Stages of Vocational Awareness," in *To Build the Life You Want, Create the Work You Love* (New York: St. Martin's Press, 1995), 14-5.

Chapter 2: Working from the Heart

1. Gloria Steinem, *Revolution from Within* (New York: Little, Brown, 1992).
2. Richard Nelson Bolles, *How to Find Your Mission in Life* (Berkeley, Calif.: Ten Speed Press, 1991), 2, 6, 10.
3. Franklin Graham with Jeanette Lockerbie, *Bob Pierce: This One Thing I Do* (Waco, Tex.: Word, 1983), 77.
4. Frederick Buechner, *Wishful Thinking: A Theological ABC* (New York: Harper & Row, 1973), 95.

5. Jean Blomquist, "Discovering Our Deep Gladness: The Healing Power of Work," *Weavings* 8, no. 1 (1993): 24.
6. Thomas Kelly, *A Testament of Devotion* (New York: Walker and Co., 1987), 149-50.
7. Ethel May Baldwin and David V. Benson, *Henrietta Mears and How She Did It!* (Glendale, Calif.: Gospel Light Publications, 1966), 83. Copyright © 1966, 1980. Used by permission of Regal Books, Ventura, CA 93003.
8. Baldwin and Benson, *Henrietta Mears,* 142-3.

Chapter 3: Misconceptions about Purpose

1. Bill Stearns, *Catch the Vision!* brochure for IFMA Frontier Peoples Committee, 1990, inside page.
2. Buechner, *Wishful Thinking,* 95.
3. Adapted from Gloria Steinem, *Revolution from Within* (Boston: Little, Brown, 1992), 268.
4. John Woolman, *The Journal of John Woolman* (New York: Corinth Books, 1961), vi, xi.
5. Woolman, *The Journal of John Woolman,* 180-1.
6. Quoted in Madeleine L'Engle, *Walking on Water: Reflections on Faith and Art* (Wheaton, Ill.: Harold Shaw, 1980), 132.

Chapter 4: The Feminine Edge of Purpose

1. I am indebted to Ruth Tucker for these observations; see *Daughters of the Church* (Grand Rapids, Mich.: Zondervan, 1987), 20.
2. *World Vision,* Special Issue on Girls, April-May 1998, 9-10, 13.
3. Miriam quoted this to me from "Ministering Women" (interview discussion with four Christian leaders), *Christianity Today,* 8 April 1996, 16, 19-20.
4. Lisa DiMona and Constance Herndon, eds., *The 1995 Information Please Women's Sourcebook* (Boston: Houghton Mifflin, 1994), 421.
5. May Sarton, introduction to *The Russia House* by John LeCarre (New York: Knopf, 1989), quoted in Jim Wallis, *The Soul of Politics* (New York: The New Press; Maryknoll, N.Y.: Orbis Books, 1994), 140.
6. Bill and Kathy Peel, *Discover Your Destiny* (Colorado Springs, Colo.: NavPress, 1996), 25.
7. This paraphrases Mordecai's words to his cousin, Queen Esther: "Who knoweth whether thou art come to the kingdom for such a time as this?" (Esther 4:14, KJV).
8. Miriam Adeney, *A Time for Risking* (Portland, Oreg.: Multnomah, 1987), 12. Available only from Christian Book Distributors, Peabody, Mass. Used by permission of the author.
9. Evelyn Underhill, *Selections from the Writings of Evelyn Underhill,* ed. Douglas Steere (Nashville, Tenn.: The Upper Room, 1961), 10.

Chapter 5: Linking Up with God's Purposes

1. Victor Hugo, *Les Misérables* (Greenwich, Conn.: Fawcette Books, 1961), 39.
2. *Union Signal,* 22 April 1886, and "Does God Speak to Women?" *West Bluff Word* (Ill.), November 1983, as quoted in Ruth Hoppin, "The Legacy of Katherine Bushnell," *Priscilla Papers* 9 (Winter 1995): 8-9.
3. Judith Papachristou, *Women Together: A History in Documents of the Women's Movement in the United States* (New York: Knopf, 1976), 4, and Gerda Lerner, *The Grimke Sisters from South Carolina: Pioneers for Women's Rights and Abolition* (New York: Shocken Books, 1971), 7, quoted in Ruth Tucker, "Four Seasons of Women's Ministries" (paper presented at the Women's Ministries Institute Symposium, Pasadena, Calif., March 24, 1995), p. 35 of symposium syllabus.
4. Available from US Center for World Mission, 1605 Elizabeth St., Pasadena, CA 91104.
5. Dallas Willard, *The Divine Conspiracy* (San Francisco: HarperSanFrancisco, 1998), 121.
6. Willard, *The Divine Conspiracy,* 123-4.
7. Willard, *The Divine Conspiracy*, 124.

Chapter 6: Looking for Clues

1. Introduced to me by art and psychological therapists Mary Braheny and Diane Halperin, Manhattan Beach, Calif.
2. Henri Nouwen, *Life of the Beloved* (New York: Crossroad, 1995), 87-8.
3. Jean Blomquist, "Discovering Our Deep Gladness: The Healing Power of Work," *Weavings* 8, no.1 (1993): 25.
4. As quoted in Gail Sheehy, *New Passages* (New York: Ballantine Books, 1995), 233.
5. U.S. Department of Education, National Center for Education Statistics, Integrated Postsecondary Education Data System's "Fall Enrollment, 1991 Survey," by Evelyn Mann, Table 17, as quoted in Sheehy, *New Passages,* 412.
6. Frederick Buechner, *Wishful Thinking: A Theological ABC* (New York: Harper & Row, 1973), 95.
7. Patricia Daniels Cornwell, *A Time for Remembering: The Ruth Bell Graham Story* (Minneapolis: Grason, 1983), x, 27, 157-8, 168, 228.

Chapter 7: The Stages of Discovery

1. From Dr. Herman J. Aafrtink's lecture, The Paraclete, QF #488, available from Calgary Life Enrichment Centre, Calgary, Alberta, Canada, as quoted in Marsha Sinetar, *To Build the Life You Want, Create the Work You Love* (New York: St. Martin's Press, 1995), 43.
2. RuthAnn Ridley, "Beyond Time," *Discipleship Journal* 28 (1985), 39-40.
3. Parker Palmer, "On Minding Your Call—When No One Is Calling," *Weavings* 11, no. 3 (1996): 19.
4. Palmer, "Minding Your Call," 18.

5. As quoted in Sheehy, *New Passages*, xvi.

6. Baldwin and Benson, *Henrietta Mears,* 62.

7. Devid W. Bebbington, "Elizabeth Fry and Prison Reform," in *Great Leaders of the Christian Faith,* ed. John Woodbridge (Chicago: Moody, 1988), 314, as quoted in Tucker, "Four Seasons of Women's Ministries," p. 34 of symposium syllabus.

8. Janet Whitney, *Elizabeth Fry: Quaker Heroine* (Boston: Little, Brown, 1936), 220, as quoted in Tucker, "Four Seasons of Women's Ministries," p. 35 of symposium syllabus.

9. Sinetar, *To Build the Life You Want,* 55.

Chapter 8: Stating Your Mission

1. Christine Aroney-Sine, *Tales of a Seasick Doctor* (Grand Rapids, Mich.: Zondervan, 1996), 124.

2. Laurie Beth Jones, *The Path: Creating Your Mission Statement for Work and for Life* (New York: Hyperion Press, 1996), 3.

3. For example, Stephen Covey describes the "personal mission statement" as a personal philosophy or creed. One example includes seventeen maxims about living (e.g., "Succeed at home first") and another is a seven-paragraph statement of all the things a person wants to do. Stephen Covey, *The 7 Habits of Highly Effective People* (New York: Simon & Schuster, 1989), 106-7.

4. Richard Nelson Bolles, *How to Find Your Mission in Life* (Berkeley, Calif.: Ten Speed Press, 1991), 50-1.

5. Ruth Tucker, *Daughters of the Church* (Grand Rapids, Mich.: Zondervan, 1987), 272-3. Copyright © 1987 by Ruth A. Tucker & Walter L. Liefeld. Used by permission of Zondervan Publishing House.

6. Tucker, *Daughters of the Church,* 272-4.

7. *International Standard Bible Encyclopedia,* s.v. "David." Together, this report of Josephus and the biblical record make it appear that David was a teenager when anointed king, about thirty when he became king of Judah, and thirty-seven when he became king over all Israel.

8. W. J. Weatherby, *Chariots of Fire* (New York: Dell/Quicksilver, 1981), 16, 86-7, as quoted in Sinetar, *To Build the Life You Want,* 168.

Chapter 9: A Heart for God

1. Baldwin and Benson, *Henrietta Mears,* 57.

2. Baldwin and Benson, *Henrietta Mears,* 276-7.

3. Robert Anthony, *Doing What You Love, Loving What You Do* (New York: Berkeley Books, 1991), 16-7.

4. Julian of Norwich, *Selections from the Revelations of Divine Love,* ed. Constance Garrett, Great Devotional Classics (Nashville, Tenn.: The Upper Room, 1963), 20.

5. Richard Foster, *Prayer: Finding the Heart's True Home* (San Francisco: HarperSanFrancisco, 1992), 70.

6. Jim Wallis, *The Soul of Politics* (New York: Orbis Books, 1994), 196, 200.

7. Henri Nouwen, *The Way of the Heart* (San Francisco: HarperSanFrancisco, 1991), 37.

8. Dallas Willard, *In Search of Guidance: Developing a Conversational Relationship with God* (San Francisco: HarperSanFrancisco, 1993), 239.

9. Basil Pennington, "The Call to Contemplation," *Weavings* 11, no. 3 (1996): 36.

10. Vincent van Gogh, *The Letters of Vincent van Gogh,* ed. Mark Roskill (New York: Atheneum, 1963), 110.

Chapter 10: Not Enough Confidence...Too Much Confidence

1. Baldwin and Benson, *Henrietta Mears,* 114.

2. William Johnston, ed., *The Cloud of Unknowing* (New York: Image Books, 1973), 66.

3. John Henry Newman, as quoted in *Renovare Perspective* 4 (July 1994).

Chapter 11: Nurturing God-Empowered Passion

1. Sinetar, *To Build the Life You Want,* 120-1.

2. Michael Wallach and Nathan Kogan, "Sex Differences and Judgment Processes," *Journal of Personality and Social Psychology* 27, no. 4 (1959): 561, as quoted in Joanne Wilkens, *Her Own Business: Success Secrets of Entrepreneurial Women* (New York: McGraw-Hill, 1987), 21.

3. Wilkens, *Her Own Business,* 21.

4. Tucker, *Daughters of the Church,* 305.

5. Tucker, *Daughters of the Church,* 305-6.

6. This theme is fleshed out in Walter Brueggemann, *The Prophetic Imagination* (Philadelphia: Fortress, 1978), 44-108.

7. Wendy M. Wright, "Wisdom of the Mothers," *Weavings* 12, no. 4 (1997): 9-10.

8. Tucker, *Daughters of the Church,* 160.

9. Tucker, *Daughters of the Church,* 160.

10. Brennan Manning, *Abba's Child* (Colorado Springs, Colo.: NavPress, 1994), 125.

Chapter 12: Even the Lone Ranger Had a Sidekick

1. Vincent van Gogh, *The Complete Letters of Vincent van Gogh,* 3 vols. (Greenwich, Conn.: New York Graphic Society, 1959), 1:197, as quoted in Henri Nouwen, *The Way of the Heart* (San Francisco: HarperSanFrancisco, 1991), 55.

2. Carol Gilligan, *In a Different Voice: Psychological Theory and Women's Development* (Cambridge, Mass.: Harvard University Press, 1983), 49, 62, as quoted in Wilkens, *Her Own Business,* 126.

3. Willa Cather, *O Pioneers!* (New York: Vintage Books, 1992), 25.

4. Tucker, *Daughters of the Church,* 250.
5. Baldwin and Benson, *Henrietta Mears,* 109.

Chapter 13: Dreaming in Purposeful Ways

1. DiMona and Herndon, *The 1995 Information Please Women's Sourcebook,* 422.
2. Paraphrased from Adeney, *A Time for Risking,* 56.

Chapter 14: Bring Your Brokenness to God

1. Sheehy, *New Passages,* 120-121.
2. Basil Pennington, "The Call to Contemplation," *Weavings* 11, no. 3 (1996): 35.
3. Pennington, "The Call to Contemplation," 35.
4. Foster, *Prayer: Finding the Heart's True Home,* 72.
5. Eugenia Price, *Discoveries* (Grand Rapids, Mich.: Zondervan, 1970), 57.
6. Charles Olsen, *Transforming Church Boards* (New York: An Alban Institute Publication, 1995), 130.
7. For further meditation on this passage, see Jan Johnson, *Listening to God: Using Scripture as a Path to God's Presence* (Colorado Springs, Colo.: NavPress, 1998), sec. 1, meditation 1.
8. Evelyn Underhill, *Selections from the Writings of Evelyn Underhill,* ed. Douglas Steere (Nashville, Tenn.: The Upper Room, 1961), 23-4.

Chapter 15: When You Feel Like Quitting

1. Oswald Chambers, *My Utmost for His Highest: An Updated Edition in Today's Language,* ed. James Reimann (Grand Rapids, Mich.: Discovery House; Nashville, Tenn.: Nelson, 1992), May 8.
2. Johnson, *Listening to God,* 155-6.
3. From presentation by Robert Mauer, Ph.D., UCLA, "The Art and Science of Mistakes," Santa Barbara Writer's Conference, June 22, 1997.
4. Sheehy, *New Passages,* 119.
5. Baldwin and Benson, *Henrietta Mears,* 161.

Chapter 16: Moving Around the Obstacles

1. Aroney-Sine, *Tales of a Seasick Doctor,* 142.
2. Baldwin and Benson, *Henrietta Mears,* 143, 45.
3. Tucker, *Daughters of the Church,* 305.
4. Amy Carmichael, *A Very Present Help,* ed. Judith Couchman (Ann Arbor, Mich.: Servant, 1996), 32.

Chapter 17: Pulling in the People You Love Without Turning Them Off

1. Kari Torjesen Malcolm, *Women at the Crossroads* (Carol Stream, Ill.: InterVarsity, 1982), 184-5.
2. Miriam Adeney, as quoted in "Ministering Women," *Christianity Today*, 8 April 1996, 19.
3. Miriam Adeney, *A Time for Risking,* 54.

Chapter 18: Making the Trade-Offs

1. Anne Ortlund, *Disciplines of a Beautiful Woman* (Waco, Tex.: Word, 1977), 49-50.
2. Adeney, *A Time for Risking,* 47-8.
3. Henry David Thoreau, as quoted in *A Treasury of Religious Quotations,* ed. Gerald Tomlinson (Englewood Cliffs, N.J.: Prentice-Hall, 1991), 246.
4. Malcolm, *Women at the Crossroads,* 179.
5. E. Glenn Hinson, "Kindlers and Purifiers of Dreams," *Weavings* 11, no. 3 (May-June 1996): 41.
6. Gordon Dahl, *Work, Play, and Worship in a Leisure-Oriented Society* (Minneapolis: Augsburg, 1972), 12, as quoted in Tim Hansel, *When I Relax I Feel Guilty* (Elgin, Ill.: David C. Cook, 1979), 33.
7. G. K. Chesterton, *What's Wrong with the World* (New York: Dodd, Mead, 1910), as quoted in *The Quotable Chesterton,* ed. George Marlin, Richard Rabatin, and John L. Swan (Garden City, N.Y.: Image Books, 1987), 95.

Chapter 19: My Prayer for You

1. Underhill, *Selections from the Writings of Evelyn Underhill,* 6-7.
2. Bolles, *How to Find Your Mission,* 16-7.
3. Gerald Tomlinson, ed., *A Treasury of Religious Quotations* (Englewood Cliffs, N.J.: Prentice-Hall, 1991), 108.
4. Quoted in a handout from Robert Mauer, Ph.D., UCLA, "The Art and Science of Mistakes," presented at the Santa Barbara Writer's Conference, June 22, 1997, 2.
5. Carmichael, *A Very Present Help,* 75.
6. Saint Augustine, *Selections from Augustine,* ed. William Cannon, Great Devotional Classics (Nashville, Tenn.: The Upper Room, 1950), 13.

ABOUT THE AUTHOR

Jan Johnson is an award-winning author of nine books and nearly a thousand magazine articles. A member of the American Society of Journalists and Authors, she has sold articles to *Woman's Day, Parenting,* the *Los Angeles Times,* and the *Chicago Tribune.* She also has written for Christian magazines such as *Discipleship Journal, Christianity Today, Focus on the Family, Virtue, World Vision,* and *Weavings.*

When she's not writing, Jan enjoys speaking at retreats, conferences, and luncheons, hoping to ignite within listeners a burning desire to know God in an authentic way. She holds degrees in Christian education and biblical studies, and has led many discipleship groups, recovery groups, and writing classes.

She resides in Southern California with her husband, Greg, and their two teenagers, Jeff and Janae.